# taste.
# COMFORT FOOD

Over 100 mouth-watering recipes

**igloo**

# igloo

Published in 2010
by Igloo Books Ltd
Cottage Farm
Sywell
NN6 0BJ

www.igloo-books.com
Copyright © 2010 Igloo Books Ltd

10 9 8 7 6 5 4 3 2
ISBN: 978 1 84852 843 7

Food photography and recipe development: Stockfood, The Food Image Agency
Front and back cover images © Stockfood, The Food Image Agency

Printed and manufactured in China.

# contents.

# introduction.

Whoever we are, there is always a time when we yearn for food that fills us with contentment – comfort food. The recipes in this book offer the satisfaction which we all crave at some time, and more often than we might think! Whether you've had a bad day at work, feeling a bit under the weather, or if it's cold and rainy outside, nothing is more comforting than good, home-cooked food.

Comfort food can be quite difficult to define, but everyone instinctively knows exactly what it means – that's because it tends to mean different things to different people. Obviously, it is something that is fairly simple to cook, yet it is generous, full of flavour and satisfyingly tasty, maybe even wickedly indulgent. It is often a dish that has nostalgic associations, generally of childhood, family warmth and mother's indulgence.

The recipes in this book are not only mouth-watering, but deeply satisfying too and there is also a great choice for vegetarians in every section. Some of the recipes also have a strong cultural element. For instance, comfort food for a Moroccan would probably be a slow-cooked chicken tagine with olives and lemons, while someone from Mexico may long for chilli con carne. Greeks might dream of stifado, and Italians, pasta. All of these dishes provide a sense of comfort and well-being and in the following pages we offer a selection of both hearty, and lighter, food from around the world.

Soup is an ultimate comfort food; lift your spirits with a luxurious bowl of cauliflower and Roquefort, or take a bit of extra time to create your own lobster bisque – the ultimate in soup heaven, not forgetting, of course, chicken noodle, the universal soup-boost. The texture of sweet potato and thick vegetable soup is akin to a warm blanket wrapped around you on a cold day. Soups are easy to prepare and can be a meal in themselves, when time, or effort, isn't readily available. There is also a selection of quick and easy recipes which could double-up as light supper, or lunch dishes.

For something a little more substantial, the main course section is bursting with delicious ideas, both traditional and with some new and exciting recipes to try. For those who have always loved Mum's shepherd's pie, but didn't know how to make it, the recipe in this book is easy and straightforward, with a result your mum would be proud of. Casseroles and hot-pots are great for a cold winter's evening, and the pastas and the fish dishes are great for a summer evening when nothing else will do.

The mouth-watering rice and pasta dishes are so versatile they can either be eaten as a meal in themselves, or alongside another of the succulent mains. Imagine serving a Greek pilaf with a hearty stifado – wow! Pasta and rice dishes are great for sharing with friends and so quick and easy to put together when unexpected guests arrive.

When we think of comfort food our thoughts often drift to puddings. Remember the desserts we enjoyed as children? Mum's bread and butter pudding, rhubarb crumble, banoffee pie and homemade sticky toffee pudding. Well, they are all in here, and more. Sometimes, only a sweet treat will 'hit the spot' and there are so many to choose from. A summer barbeque wouldn't be complete without strawberry shortcake, or a chocolate mousse. A Sunday lunch in November needs an apple pie.

The warm, inner glow a luscious dessert leaves behind is recommendation in itself.

What is perhaps most important about comfort food is the enjoyment and pleasure we derive from cooking and eating it. It can lift the most terrible of moods and help to soothe and placate the mind. The methodical processes involved in cooking help us to relax and unwind after a stressful day at work. What's even better are the results we have to show for all our hard work – a delicious, homemade indulgence that makes everything seem just that little bit better.

Nothing compares to Comfort Food.

soups
& stews.

# Tomato soup

**Prep and cook time: 45 minutes**
**Can be frozen**
**Serves: 4**

**Ingredients:**
3 tbsp olive oil
2 onions, chopped
2 cloves garlic, chopped
1 red chilli pepper, deseeded, chopped
400 g | 2 cups tomatoes, chopped
200 g | 1 cup pureed tomatoes
600 ml | 2 ½ cups vegetable stock
2 tbsp fresh basil, chopped
1 tbsp fresh parsley, chopped
3 tbsp balsamic vinegar
½ tsp sugar
Tabasco
4 tbsp crème fraiche

**To garnish:**
chives, chopped
extra virgin olive oil

**Method:**
Heat the oil in a large pan. Fry the onion, garlic
and chilli pepper, stirring.

Add the chopped and pureed tomatoes. Pour on the stock.
Stir in the basil, parsley and balsamic vinegar.
Season with salt, sugar and 1-2 dashes Tabasco.

Let the soup simmer over a medium heat for 20-25 minutes,
stirring occasionally.

Puree and sieve the soup. Return to the pan, bring to a boil,
stir in the creme fraiche and check the seasoning.

Serve garnished with chopped chives and drizzled with
a little extra virgin olive oil.

# Stifado – beef stew with onions and tomatoes

**Prep and cook time: 2 hours 30 minutes**
**Can be frozen**
**Serves: 4**

**Ingredients:**
800 g | 2 lbs beef,
from the leg, de-boned
3 tbsp olive oil
2 cloves garlic
3 bay leaves
1 cinnamon stick
½ tsp nutmeg, ground
½ tsp cumin, ground
1 tbsp tomato paste
2 tbsp red wine vinegar
250 g | 1 cup canned tomatoes
100 ml | 7 tbsp dry red wine
400 g | 2 cups rice
600 g | 1 ½ lbs small onions
400 g | 1 lb small tomatoes
2 tbsp parsley, chopped

**Method:**
Wash the beef, pat dry and cut into 2 cm cubes, and coat lightly in flour. Heat the oil in a large pot and fry the meat until browned on all sides. Season with salt and pepper then take out of the pan.

Peel and finely chop the garlic. Put the garlic, bay leaf, cinnamon stick, nutmeg, cinnamon, cumin and tomato paste in the fat and sauté, stirring continually.

Put the meat back in the pan and stir. Pour in the red wine vinegar and simmer for 2-3 minutes. Now add the canned tomatoes and 2 cups of water, enough to just cover the meat. Pour in the wine, cover with a lid and simmer for 1 hour.

Put the small onions in boiling water and leave for about 1 minute. Drain, put under cold water and peel. Put the onions in the pan and simmer for another 1 hour.

Put the small tomatoes in the pot about 15 minutes before serving. Season to taste and stir in the chopped parsley. Serve with rice.

# Broccoli and chive soup

**Prep and cook time: 30 minutes**
**Can be frozen**
**Serves: 4 as a starter, 2 as a main**

**Ingredients:**
2 tbsp olive oil
3 shallots, finely chopped
1 clove garlic, finely chopped
300 g 1 ¾ cups broccoli florets
600 ml | 2 ½ cups vegetable stock
a handful of chives, chopped,
save a few to garnish
3 tbsp crème fraiche
1 dash lemon juice

**Method:**
Heat the oil in a pan and fry the shallot and garlic until soft. Add the broccoli and pour on the stock. Simmer for 20 minutes.

Add the chopped chives, reserving a few to garnish. Puree the soup. Stir in the crème fraiche and season with salt, pepper and lemon juice.

Garnish with the remaining chives and serve.

# Fish chowder

**Prep and cook time: 30 minutes**
**Can be frozen**
**Serves: 4**

**Ingredients:**
2 tbsp butter
1 onion, chopped
2 cloves garlic, chopped
200 g | ½ lb celeriac|celery root, chopped
2 tbsp plain|all purpose flour
800 ml | 3 ½ cups fish stock
400 g | 1 lb smoked trout fillets, skinned
200 ml | ⅞ cup cream
1 tbsp lemon juice

**Method:**
Heat the butter in a pan and fry the onion, garlic and celeriac/celery root gently for 2 minutes. Add the flour and pour on the fish stock. Tear 200 g of the trout into pieces and add to the soup with the cream.

Simmer gently for 20 minutes, stirring occasionally.

Puree the soup finely and season with salt, ground pepper and lemon juice.

Spoon the soup into bowls. Tear the remaining trout into pieces and place them in the soup. Garnish with ground black pepper and dill sprigs and serve.

# Cauliflower and Roquefort soup

**Prep and cook time: 30 minutes**
**Can be frozen**
**Serves: 4**

**Ingredients:**
600 g | 3 ½ cups cauliflower florets
600 ml | 2 ½ cups vegetable stock
150 g | ⅔ cup crème fraiche
Salt & freshly ground pepper
2000 ml | 8 cups bread, stale
1 tbsp butter
ground nutmeg
200 g | 2 cups Roquefort cheese
1 tbsp finely chopped parsley

**Method:**

Put the vegetable stock into a pan, bring to the boil, add the cauliflower and simmer gently for 20 minutes. Then puree the soup, stir in the crème fraiche, season with salt and pepper and add nutmeg to taste.

Dice the bread and fry in butter until golden brown. Take out of the pan and drain on paper towels.

Crumble the Roquefort into 4 bowls and ladle the hot soup into the bowls. Garnish with a little freshly ground pepper, parsley and the croutons and serve.

# Chorizo stew with soured cream and parsley

**Prep and cook time: 1 hour**
**Can be frozen**
**Serves: 4**

**Ingredients:**
2 red onions
4 cloves garlic
250 g | ½ lb chorizo
400 g | 1 lb waxy potatoes, diced
1 red bell pepper, chopped
1 yellow bell pepper, chopped
1 small carrot, chopped
1 stalk celery, chopped
2 carrots, chopped
3 tbsp olive oil
400 g | 2 cups tomatoes, chopped
1000 ml | 4 cups vegetable stock
1 bay leaf
1-2 tsp dried oregano
200 g | 1 cup chickpeas|garbanzo beans
1 tbsp soured cream

**Method:**
Cut the onion in half, then into slices. Chop the garlic. Cut the chorizo sausage into slices.

Fry the chorizo sausage in olive oil, then add the onions and the garlic and sauté until soft.

Add the vegetables and pour in the vegetable stock. Season with salt, pepper, bay leaf and oregano. Cover with a lid and simmer gently for 30 minutes on a low heat.

Drain the chickpeas/garbanzo beans, then add to the stew and heat. Season with salt and pepper and serve with a spoonful of soured cream.

# Mushroom soup with a puff pastry crust

**Prep and cook time: 1 hour**
**Cannot be frozen**
**Serves: 4 (4 ovenproof soup dishes)**

**Ingredients:**
2 shallots
1 tbsp butter
500 g | 1 ¼ lb button mushrooms
2 tsp lemon juice
500 ml | 2 cups vegetable stock
150 g | ½ cup crème fraiche
20 g | 1 cup parsley
250 g | ½ lb puff pastry,
thawed if frozen
2 egg yolks

**Method:**
Heat the oven to 220°C (180°C fan) 425°F, gas 7.

Peel and finely chop the shallots and sweat in butter until translucent. Clean the mushrooms, reserve half and roughly chop the rest. Sprinkle with lemon juice.

Add the chopped mushrooms to the shallots and sweat until the liquid has evaporated. Puree finely and mix with the vegetable stock.

Return to the pan and bring to a boil briefly, then stir in the crème fraiche and season with salt and pepper.

Thinly slice the reserved mushrooms, finely chop the parsley and add both to the soup.

Roll out the puff pastry and cut four circles 4 cm / 1½" bigger than the soup dishes.

Whisk the egg yolks and brush the outer rim of each soup dish with egg yolk. Lay the pastry circles on top of the cups (don't pull them too taut) and press the pastry firmly onto the rims.

Cut out shapes from the pastry scraps and place on the pastry lids. Brush with the remaining egg yolk.

Put the dishes on a baking sheet and bake for 15-20 minutes, until golden brown. Serve immediately.

# Fish stew with potatoes

**Prep and cook time: 1 hour**
**Cannot be frozen**
**Serves: 4**

**Ingredients:**

2 tbsp olive oil

2 onions, finely chopped

2 cloves garlic, finely chopped

1-2 small red chillies, deseeded
and finely chopped

a pinch of saffron threads

400 g | 2 cups tomatoes, chopped

1 tbsp tomato paste

200 ml | $^7/_8$ cup dry white wine

400 g | 1 lb waxy potatoes,
peeled and diced

sea salt and pepper

350 g | 1 lb mixed seafood
(prawns, mussels, squid)

600 g | 1 $^1/_2$ lb fish fillets of your choice

1 tbsp parsley, chopped

**Method:**

Heat the olive oil in a large skillet. Fry the onions, garlic, chilli and saffron threads over a medium heat for 10 minutes.

Add the tomatoes, tomato paste and white wine.
Bring to a boil, then reduce the heat and simmer for 5 minutes.

Add the potatoes and simmer gently for 20 minutes.
Season with salt and pepper.

Wash and clean the seafood and fish fillets and add the seafood to the soup. Place the fish fillets on the top.

Cover and simmer for a further 10-15 minutes over a medium heat. Spoon into 4 bowls, sprinkle with freshly chopped parsley and serve.

# French onion soup

**Prep and cook time: 1 hour 20 minutes**
**Cannot be frozen**
**Serves: 6**

**Ingredients:**
**For the soup:**
**3 tbsp butter, cut into 3 pieces**
**6 large onions (about 4 lbs), halved and cut into ¼" thick slices**
**500 ml | 2 cups water**
**125 ml | ½ cup dry sherry or dry red wine**
**1000 ml | 4 cups chicken stock**
**500 ml | 2 cups beef stock**
**6 g fresh thyme, tied with kitchen twine**
**1 bay leaf**
**½ teaspoon salt**
**2 tbsp cornflour|cornstarch**

**For cheese croutons:**
**1 small French stick, cut into ½" slices**
**200 g | 2 ½ cups Gruyère cheese, grated**

**Method:**

Melt the butter in a large pan and add the peeled and thinly sliced onions.

Cover and cook over low heat for 15 minutes, then remove the cover and cook until they are golden brown, stirring occasionally. Be careful not to over-caramelize them as they will make the soup taste bitter.

Stir in 2 cups water, wine, stocks, thyme, bay leaf, and ½ teaspoon salt, scraping up any final bits of browned crust on bottom and sides of pot. Increase heat to high and bring to simmer.

Reduce heat to low, cover and simmer for 30 minutes. Remove and discard herbs, then season with salt and pepper.

In a small bowl, mix the cornflour with about 1/4 cup water until thoroughly blended. Add this mixture to the soup and stir until it comes back up to the boil. Simmer for a few minutes until the soup has thickened, then remove from heat.

For the croutons:

Heat oven to 200°C (180°C fan) 400°F, gas 6.

While soup simmers, arrange bread slices in single layer on baking sheet and bake until crisp and golden at edges, about 10 minutes. Set aside.

Set individual grill-safe crocks on baking a sheet and fill each dish. Top each bowl with one or two bread slices (do not overlap slices) and sprinkle evenly with Gruyère.

Bake gently for 5 minutes until the cheese has melted and the bread is toasty.

# Lamb goulash with string beans in beer sauce

**Prep and cook time: 1 hour 50 minutes**
**Can be frozen**
**Serves: 4**

**Ingredients:**
**2 tbsp oil**
**800 g | 2 lbs shoulder of lamb, trimmed, chopped into bite-sized pieces**
**2 onions, finely chopped**
**2 tbsp tomato paste**
**400 ml | 1²/₃ cups light beer**
**200 g | ½ lb green | string beans**
**100 g | ½ cup dried apricots, sliced**
**1 tsp caraway seeds**

**Method:**
Heat the oil in a pan and fry the lamb all over.
Add the onions and fry until golden brown.

Stir in the tomato paste, pour on the beer and simmer gently for 1½ hours, stirring occasionally. Add a little more beer if necessary.

Blanch the beans in boiling salted water for 8 minutes. Drain and rinse under cold water.

Add the apricots and beans 10 minutes before serving. Season the goulash with salt, ground pepper and caraway and serve.

# Pumpkin and potato soup

**Prep and cook time: 50 minutes**
**Can be frozen**
**Serves: 4**

**Ingredients:**
**500 g | 1¼ lbs potatoes**
**1 onion**
**1 tbsp oil**
**500 g | 1¼ lbs pumpkin, or winter squash, sliced (prepared weight)**
**1 litre | 4 cups vegetable stock**
**nutmeg**
**50 ml | 10 tsp cream**
**1 tsp curry powder, hot**

**Method:**

Wash the potatoes. Peel and roughly dice the onion and potatoes.

Heat the oil in a large pan and sweat the onion until translucent.

Add the pumpkin and potatoes and sweat for 5 minutes. Add the stock and a little nutmeg. Bring to the boil, stirring, cover and simmer for 30 minutes.

Puree the soup finely, adding a little more broth if the soup is too thick. Add cream, curry powder, nutmeg, salt and pepper to taste.

Ladle on to warmed soup plates and serve.

# Chicken noodle soup with vegetables

**Prep and cook time: 30 minutes**
**Can be frozen**
**Serves: 4**

**Ingredients:**
**1 red bell pepper, deseeded and diced**
**250 g | 1½ cups asparagus tips**
**600 g | 1½ lbs or 4 chicken breasts**
**1 onion, chopped**
**2 cloves garlic, chopped**
**1 tbsp butter**
**100 g | 1 cup tubetti noodles,**
**or similar soup noodles**
**1000 ml | 4 cups chicken stock**
**150 ml | ⅔ cup dry white wine**
**200 g | 1 cup canned corn**
**Cayenne pepper**
**2 tbsp white wine vinegar**

**Method:**

Heat the butter in a pan and gently fry the onion and garlic until translucent.

Add the wine and the stock, bring it to the boil and simmer for 5 minutes.

Dice the chicken breasts and add to the soup with the bell pepper, asparagus and corn.

Cook for a further 10 minutes, season to taste with salt, Cayenne pepper and vinegar and serve immediately.

# Sweet potato soup with lentils and balsamic onions

**Prep and cook time: 50 minutes**
**Can be frozen**
**Serves: 4**

**Ingredients:**
1 onion
450 g | 1 lb sweet potatoes
1 leek
100 g | ½ cup red lentils
2 tbsp butter
1 clove garlic
1 tsp ground coriander
1000 ml | 4 cups vegetable stock
2 tbsp snipped chives
2 red onions
1 tbsp butter
4 tbsp balsamic vinegar

**Method:**

Peel and finely dice the onion. Peel and chop the sweet potatoes. Wash, trim and chop the leek. Wash the lentils under running water.

Heat the butter and sauté the onion until translucent, press in the garlic and sauté gently for a few minutes.

Stir in the coriander, then add the sweet potatoes and leek and sauté, stirring, for 5 minutes.

Add the vegetable stock and the lentils, cover and simmer for 30 minutes.

Meanwhile peel and slice the red onions and sauté in butter until soft. Add the balsamic vinegar and simmer until slightly reduced.

Remove the soup from the heat, season to taste, stir in the chives and ladle into plates or bowls. Serve garnished with balsamic onions.

# Irish stew

**Prep and cook time: 2 hours 50 minutes**
**Can be frozen**
**Serves: 4**

**Ingredients:**
**400 g | 1 lb waxy potatoes, diced**
**300 g | ¾ lb waxy potatoes,**
**sliced very thinly**
**4 carrots, finely chopped**
**3 onions, sliced**
**800 g | 2 lbs lean lamb, diced**
**1 tsp chopped thyme**
**250ml | ⅔ cup lamb stock**

**Method:**

Heat the oven to 180°C (160°C fan) 375°F, gas 5.

Put half of the diced potatoes into a wide ovenproof casserole, then add half of the onions and carrots. Add the meat and season with salt and pepper.

Scatter half of the thyme over the meat. Now add the rest of the diced potatoes and onions and finish with the rest of the carrots. Season well with salt and pepper.

Add the stock to cover the potatoes. Bring to the boil, then cook the casserole in the oven with a lid on for 2½ hours.

30 minutes before the end of cooking time, remove the lid and arrange the sliced potatoes neatly on top of the casserole. Scatter with the rest of the thyme leaves and season with salt and pepper.

Return the casserole to the oven, without the lid, for the remaining 30 minutes. The potatoes should be cooked and nicely browned.

# Creamed lobster soup

**Prep and cook time: 40 minutes**
**Can be frozen**
**Serves: 4**

**Ingredients:**
1 lobster, cooked
1 tsp ground paprika
40 g ¼ cup butter
2 tbsp plain|all purpose flour
800 ml | 3½ cups lobster stock,
or fish stock
4 tbsp lobster butter
Cayenne pepper
2-3 tbsp fish sauce
2 tbsp brandy
200 ml | ⅞ cup cream
butter

**Method:**

Break off the lobster's claws and break open with the back of a chopper. Halve the body lengthways to the tail.

Extract the lobster meat from the shell, claws and tail. Wash it, pat dry and sprinkle with a little salt and paprika.

Melt half the butter in a pan. Add the flour, stir and cook briefly. Gradually stir in the lobster stock or fish stock and bring to the boil. Mix in the lobster butter with a balloon whisk.

Heat the soup again but do not boil. Season with salt, Cayenne, fish sauce and brandy.

Add the lobster meat (apart from the tail meat) and heat through for 4 minutes. Add the cream and puree.

Heat the remaining butter. Chop the tail meat into slices and fry. Place the meat into bowls and spoon the soup over it.

# Potato goulash with pork

**Prep and cook time: 1 hour**
**Can be frozen**
**Serves: 4**

**Ingredients:**
**600 g | 1¹/₂ lbs pork, belly or neck; cubed**
**1 tsp caraway seeds, crushed**
**2 cloves garlic, chopped**
**2 tbsp paprika, sweet**
**1 kg | 2¹/₄ lbs waxy potatoes, peeled and washed**
**2 large onions, diced**
**2 tbsp butter**
**2 tbsp vinegar**
**700 ml | 3 cups meat stock**
**400 g | 2 cups tomatoes, chopped**
**4 tbsp soured cream**
**2 tbsp chopped chives**

**Method:**

Mix the meat with the salt, pepper, caraway, garlic and 1 tbsp paprika.

Heat the butter in a large skillet or pan and brown the meat on all sides over a high heat.

Add the onions and fry briefly. Sprinkle with the rest of the paprika, then immediately add the vinegar, stock, tomatoes and potatoes.

Cook over a low heat 35 minutes.

Dish the potato goulash onto plates, add a spoonful of sour cream to each and serve sprinkled with chives.

# Thick vegetable soup with corn and bacon

**Prep and cook time: 40 minutes**
**Can be frozen**
**Serves: 4**

**Ingredients:**
2 tbsp butter
1 carrot, chopped into sticks
150 g | 1½ cups celery stalk, sliced
1 clove garlic, finely chopped
1 onion, chopped
200 g | ½ lb floury potatoes, peeled and chopped
1 tbsp cornflour|cornstarch
1 dash white wine
800 ml | 3½ cups chicken stock
100 g | 1 cup canned corn
4 slices bacon, chopped
100 ml | 7 tbsp cream
1 dash lemon juice
2 tbsp fresh parsley, chopped

**Method:**
Heat the butter in a pan. Add the carrot, celery stalk, garlic, onion, potato and bacon and fry gently for a few minutes, until they begin to brown.

Add the white wine and stock and simmer for 20 minutes, stirring occasionally.

Dissolve the cornflour/cornstarch in a little water and stir into the soup with the corn and cream. Cook for 5 minutes. Season with salt, lemon juice and ground pepper.

Sprinkle with parsley and serve.

# Mulligatawny soup with chicken

**Prep and cook time: 50 minutes**
**Can be frozen**
**Serves: 4**

**Ingredients:**
3 tbsp ghee
2 cloves garlic, chopped
1 tsp fresh ginger, peeled and grated
400 g | 1 lb chicken breasts,
chopped into chunks
1 tsp ground caraway
1 tsp ground coriander
1 tsp curry powder
1 tsp turmeric
1 litre | 4 cups chicken stock
200 g | 1 cup red lentils, rinsed
Cayenne pepper
nutmeg
1 tbsp lemon juice

**To garnish:**
coriander|cilantro leaves

**Method:**
Heat the ghee in a pan and fry the garlic and ginger gently. Add the chicken and fry for 2 minutes.

Add the caraway, coriander, curry powder and turmeric and fry briefly.

Pour on the stock and add the lentils. Bring to a boil and simmer over a low heat for 30 minutes until the lentils are very soft. Stir occasionally.

Season with salt, Cayenne pepper, nutmeg and lemon juice. Garnish with coriander/cilantro leaves and serve.

# Fagiolata – bean soup with pasta

**Prep and cook time: 1 hour**
**Cannot be frozen**
**Serves: 4**

## Ingredients:

1 large white onion, chopped
400 g | 2 cups tomatoes, chopped
1 stalk celery, chopped
400 g | 2½ cups kidney beans, canned
250 g | 1 lb sedanini, or any short, tubular pasta
4 tbsp olive oil
20 g | 1 cup fresh basil leaves
20 g | 1 cup fresh parsley leaves
2 tbsp freshly grated Parmesan cheese

## Method:

Heat 4 tablespoons oil in a pan and sauté the onion until translucent. Add the tomatoes and celery stalk, cover and cook over a medium heat for 4-5 minutes.

Add enough water to cover and cook over a medium heat for 30 minutes.

Add the basil and parsley and season with salt and pepper. Bring to a boil, add the pasta and beans and cook for 8 minutes until the pasta is done, stirring frequently.

Season to taste with salt and pepper. Serve sprinkled with freshly grated Parmesan.

quick &
easy.

# Lamb burger with blue cheese and onions

**Prep and cook time: 45 minutes**
**Cannot be frozen**
**Serves: 4**

**Ingredients:**
2 red onions, 1 finely sliced,
1 finely chopped
1 clove garlic, finely chopped
3 stems parsley, few leaves
reserved, rest finely chopped
6 chives, finely chopped
1 slice bread, crust removed
400 g | 1 lb ground lamb
1 egg
2 - 3 tbsp vegetable oil
150 g | 4 slices Gorgonzola cheese
4 lettuce leaves
rolls to serve

**Method:**
Soften the bread in a little water. Mix the lamb with the chopped onion, garlic, egg and herbs.

Squeeze the water from the bread thoroughly and knead the bread into the lamb. Season generously with salt and pepper.

Shape the mix to 4 flat burgers. Heat the oil in a skillet and fry the burgers for 10 - 12 minutes over a medium heat, turning once.

Just before the burgers are done, lay a slice of Gorgonzola cheese on each. Cover the pan and let the cheese melt slightly.

Lay a lettuce leaf on the bottom half of each roll. Place a burger on the lettuce and the onion slices on top. Garnish with fresh parsley. Serve at once.

# Aubergine salad with harissa

**Prep and cook time: 20 minutes  Marinating time: 30 minutes**
**Cannot be frozen**
**Serves: 4**

**Ingredients:**
**800 g | 2 lbs aubergine|eggplant,**
**cut into thin slices**
**olive oil, for frying**
**2 tbsp harissa paste**

**Method:**

Heat 1 cm / ½ in oil in a skillet. Fry the aubergine/eggplant slices in batches for 3-4 minutes over a medium to high heat until golden brown. Place the aubergine/eggplant on paper towels and allow to drain.

Wipe the skillet with paper towels and heat 1 tbsp oil. Fry the harissa paste lightly for 1 minute. Add the eggplant slices and mix them quickly with the harissa paste.

Place the eggplant in a bowl, let cool and serve as a healthy vegetarian main or a side dish to lamb.

# BBQ chicken wings

**Prep and cook time: 1 hour 30 minutes**
**Can be frozen**
**Serves: 4**

**Ingredients:**
1 kg | 2¼ lbs chicken wings
5 tbsp sunflower oil
1 tsp salt
80 g | ¼ cup ketchup (catsup)
6 tbsp honey
2 lemons, juiced
1-2 tbsp soy sauce
2 cloves garlic, chopped
1 pinch hot paprika

**Method:**
Preheat the oven to 180°C (160°C fan) 375°F, gas 5.

Wash the chicken wings, pat dry and set aside.

Mix all other ingredients in a large bowl, add the chicken wings, coat well and marinade for 1 hour.

Transfer the chicken wings to a deep baking pan and put into the preheated oven for 15 minutes.

Increase the oven temperature to 200°C and cook for a further 10 minutes or until done, brushing once more with the marinade during this time.

# Potato and chickpea chilli with paprika sausage

**Prep and cook time: 50 minutes**
**Cannot be frozen**
**Serves: 4**

**Ingredients:**

2 onions, peeled and finely chopped
2 cloves garlic, crushed
150 g | 6 oz | 1 cup chorizo, peeled and sliced
300 g | 12oz tomatoes, chopped
400 g | 1 lb potatoes
2 tsp ground cumin
1 tsp paprika
a pinch of Cayenne pepper
2 chilli peppers, de-seeded and chopped
150 ml | ⅔ cup dry red wine
1 tsp balsamic vinegar
500 g | 1 ¼ lbs| 4 cups tinned chickpeas|garbanzo beans, drained

**To garnish:**
2 whole chilli peppers
2 tbsp chopped coriander|cilantro leaves

**Method:**

Wash and peel the potatoes and cut into quarters lengthwise.

Heat a large skillet and cook the onions, chorizo and garlic slices, the oil from the chorizo will fry the mix gently. Add the potatoes and fry all together for a couple of minutes. Then stir in the cumin, paprika, Cayenne pepper, chillies and tomatoes.

Add the wine and 350 ml / 1½ cups water and season with salt, pepper and vinegar. Put a lid on the pan and cook over a medium heat for 20 minutes.

Stir the chickpeas/garbanzo beans into the chilli and cook for a further 10 minutes.

Season with salt and pepper and serve scattered with fresh whole chillies and coriander/cilantro leaves.

# Bean and rice salad

**Prep and cook time: 35 minutes**
**Cannot be frozen**
**Serves: 4**

**Ingredients:**
150 g | ¾ cup long-grain rice
150 g | 1½ cups kidney beans, canned
150 g | 1½ cups butter beans, canned
2 tomatoes
½ small cucumber
2 tbsp white wine vinegar
5 tbsp seed oil
2 tbsp parsley, chopped

**Method:**

Cook the rice in boiling, lightly salted water for 12-15 minutes, making sure the pan does not boil dry, add a little more water if necessary.

Drain the kidney beans and butter beans, rinse in cold water and leave to drain thoroughly.

Drop the tomatoes into boiling water for a few seconds, skin, quarter, deseed and finely dice.

Wash the cucumber, cut in half lengthwise and scrape out the seeds with a small spoon. Finely dice the cucumber.

Mix the ingredients for the dressing from the vinegar, salt, pepper and oil. Stir in the parsley.

Put the rice, beans, tomatoes and diced cucumber into a salad bowl and combine.

# Fishcakes with cucumber salad and mashed potato

Prep and cook time: 45 minutes
Cannot be frozen
Serves: 4

Ingredients:

100 ml | 7 tbsp cream
400 g | 1 lb floury potatoes
1 cucumber, finely sliced
1 tsp sugar
4 stalks dill, chopped
100 ml | 7 tbsp soured cream
1-2 tbsp lemon juice
1 slice day-old white bread, crust cut off
600 g | 1½ lbs fish fillet, e. g. pollack;
finely chopped
1 egg
1 onion, chopped
8 stalks chives, chopped
2 tbsp clarified butter
200 ml | 7/8 cup milk
1 tbsp butter
1 pinch nutmeg

Method:

For the fish cakes, place the cream in the freezer for at least 15 minutes. Boil the potatoes in salted water for 15 minutes until soft.

Mix the cucumber slices with 1 tsp salt and the sugar and let stand. Mix the dill with the soured cream and lemon juice. Soften the bread in a little water.

Puree the fish in a blender, mixing in the chilled cream, ½ tsp salt and the egg. Squeeze the water out of the bread and quickly mix in the bread. Take the mixture out of the blender.

Mix the onion and chives into the fish mixture and season with pepper. Moisten your hands slightly and shape the mixture into 8 fish cakes.

Heat the clarified butter in a skillet. Fry the fish cakes for 5-7 minutes over a medium heat, turning over once.

Drain and mash the potatoes, adding the milk and butter. Season with salt, pepper and nutmeg. Drain the cucumber slices and mix with the dill cream.

Serve the fish cakes with the mashed potato and cucumber salad, garnished with the reserved dill sprigs.

# Quick tomato soup with cheese dumplings

**Prep and cook time: 25 minutes**
**Can be frozen**
**Serves: 4**

**Ingredients:**
**For the tomato soup:**
1 tbsp olive oil
2 shallots, finely chopped
1 clove garlic, finely chopped
½ tbsp sugar
1 tbsp light balsamic vinegar
1000 ml | 4 cups tomato juice
1 tsp dried oregano

**For the cheese dumplings:**
100 g | ½ cup quark
(low-fat soft cheese)
50 g | ½ cup Parmesan cheese,
finely grated
4 stems basil, leaves chopped
(reserve a few sprigs for decoration)
1 egg
4 tbsp dried breadcrumbs

**Method:**
For the soup, heat the olive oil in a pan and fry the shallots and garlic for 2-3 minutes over a low to medium heat until soft, stirring continuously. Sprinkle the sugar over and let caramelize slightly.

Pour on the balsamic vinegar and tomato juice. Add the oregano and season with salt and pepper. Simmer over a low heat for 8-10 minutes.

Mix the quark, Parmesan, basil, egg and breadcrumbs. Season with salt and pepper. Shape the mixture into walnut-sized balls and add them to the soup. Cook the cheese dumplings in the soup for 5 minutes over a very low heat until done.

Season the soup with salt and pepper and spoon into bowls. Garnish with the reserved basil sprigs.

# Mushrooms with blue cheese on polenta slices

**Prep and cook time: 20 minutes**
**Cannot be frozen**
**Serves: 4**

**Ingredients:**
**For the polenta:**
**150 g | 1 cup instant polenta**
**125 g | 1¼ cup Parmesan,**
**freshly grated**
**a little oil**

**For the topping:**
**200 g | 1⅔ cups medium-sized**
**button mushrooms**
**3 tbsp olive oil**
**Juice of 1 lemon**
**100 g | 1 cup blue cheese**
**2 tbsp olive oil, for grilling**
**1 handful small beetroot leaves**

**Method:**
Prepare the polenta according to the instructions on the packet. Stir in the Parmesan and spread on a cookie sheet lined with baking parchment to a thickness of 1.5 cm / ½". Leave to cool.

Clean the mushrooms, twist off the stalks and slice the caps. Heat the oil in a skillet and sauté the mushrooms for 3-4 minutes. Sprinkle with lemon juice and season with salt and pepper.

Break the blue cheese into pieces. Sort and wash the beetroot leaves and dab dry.

Cut the cooled polenta into 8 rectangles, brush with a little oil and grill on both sides under a hot grill or fry in a hot skillet.

Arrange the beetroot leaves and blue cheese attractively on the polenta slices and top with mushrooms. Season with freshly ground pepper and serve.

# Caribbean pumpkin casserole with red onions

**Prep and cook time: 30 minutes**
**Can be frozen**
**Serves: 4**

**Ingredients:**
2 tbsp light sesame oil
1 small Hokkaido pumpkin
(alternatively, use butternut squash),
de-seeded and chopped
4 red onions, cut into thin wedges
1 tsp fresh ginger, chopped
2 cloves garlic, chopped
1 red chilli, with seeds, chopped
2 tbsp brown sugar
2 limes, juice squeezed
1 orange, juice
100 ml | 7 tbsp vegetable stock
2 stalks Thai basil leaves

**Method:**

Heat the oil in a wide pan. Fry the pumpkin, onion, ginger and garlic over a high heat for 2-4 minutes, stirring. Sprinkle the sugar over and let it caramelize slightly.

Pour in the lime and orange juice. Add the stock and bring to a boil. Cover and simmer over a low heat for 12-15 minutes, until the pumpkin is cooked but still firm.

Just before serving, stir in the Thai basil leaves. Season with salt and pepper.

Arrange the pumpkin casserole in bowls, and serve with rice.

# Barbecue skewers with spicy lamb meatballs on tomato sauce

**Prep and cook time: 25 minutes**
**Can be frozen**
**Serves: 4**

**Ingredients:**
**For the skewers:**
1 slice day-old white bread, crust removed
500 g 2 lbs ground lamb
1 clove garlic, crushed
4 onions, 1 chopped, 3 in wedges
1 red chilli pepper, slit open, de-seeded and chopped
1 tbsp oil
1 egg
$\frac{1}{2}$ tsp ground cumin
$\frac{1}{2}$ tsp ground coriander
8 metal or wooden skewers
oil, for the barbecue

**For the tomato sauce:**
1 tbsp olive oil
1 clove garlic, crushed
1 tsp fresh ginger, peeled and finely chopped
1 onion, finely chopped
1 tbsp brown sugar
3 tbsp lime juice
240 g | 2 cups tomatoes, chopped
100 ml | 7 tbsp vegetable stock
4 stems coriander|cilantro, finely chopped (reserve a few leaves to garnish)

**Method:**

For the tomato sauce, heat the oil in a pan and fry the garlic, ginger and onion over a low to medium heat for 3 minutes. Sprinkle on the sugar and let caramelize slightly. Pour on the lime juice.

Add the tomatoes and the stock. Cook over a medium heat until the tomato sauce as reduced slightly. Just before the sauce is done, stir in the chopped coriander/cilantro and season with salt and pepper.

For the skewers, soften the bread in water for 3 minutes. Mix the meat in a large bowl with the garlic, onion and chilli pepper. Squeeze the water out of the bread and add the bread to the bowl. Knead in the egg with the cumin and coriander. Season generously with salt and ground pepper.

Moisten your hands and shape the mince to small balls. Thread the meatballs and the onion wedges alternately onto skewers.

Heat the barbecue. Oil the barbecue rack and lay the skewers on it. Grill for 12-15 minutes, turning once, until the meatballs are done and the onion wedges are still slightly crunchy.

Serve the skewers with the tomato sauce, garnished with the reserved coriander/cilantro leaves.

# Melba toast lasagne with mushrooms and chive cheese

**Prep and cook time: 25 minutes**
**Cannot be frozen**
**Serves: 4**

**Ingredients:**
1 small French stick, cut into 16 very thin slices
2 tbsp sunflower seeds
1 tbsp butter
1 tbsp olive oil
150 g 1¼ cups mushrooms, sliced
150 g | 1¼ cups oyster mushrooms, chopped into strips
1 shallot, finely chopped
2½ tbsp lemon juice
50 ml | 10 tsp vegetable stock
1 clove garlic, chopped
200 g | 1 cup quark (low-fat soft cheese)
2 tbsp cream
10 stalks chives, finely chopped, a few stalks reserved to garnish

**Method:**
Heat the oven to 200°C (180°C fan) 400°F, gas 6.

Lay the bread slices on a baking sheet and bake on the middle shelf for 6-8 minutes until crisp.

Roast the sunflower seeds in a wide pan for 1-2 minutes, stirring. Remove from the pan and set aside.

Heat the butter and oil in the pan. Fry the mushrooms and the shallot over a medium heat. Pour on 2 tbsp lemon juice and the stock. Season with salt and pepper and simmer until the liquid has evaporated.

Mix the garlic with the quark, cream and ½ tbsp lemon juice. Stir in the chopped chives and season with salt and pepper.

Layer the toasts, quark and mushrooms alternately on plates. Garnish with the remaining chives and sprinkle with the roast sunflower seeds.

# Gnocchi with pesto

**Prep and cook time: 40 minutes**
**Cannot be frozen**
**Serves: 4**

**Ingredients:**
**For the gnocchi:**
**800 g | 2 lbs floury potatoes, peeled and chopped**
**150 g | 1¼ cups plain|all purpose flour**
**1 egg**
**nutmeg**

**For the pesto:**
**3 tbsp pine nuts**
**80 g | 2 cups fresh basil**
**3 cloves garlic, chopped**
**80 g | ⅔ cup Parmesan cheese, freshly grated**
**100 ml | 7 tbsp olive oil**

**To garnish:**
**basil leaves**

**Method:**

For the gnocchi, cook the potatoes in salted water for 20 minutes until done. Drain and mash, allow to cool.

Mix the mashed potato with the flour and egg. Season with salt and nutmeg. The potato dough should not be sticky and should be easy to shape.

Shape the potato dough into several rolls (1½ cm / ¾" diameter) on a floured work surface. Cut into 1½ cm / ¾" pieces and shape them into little gnocchi. Place the gnocchi in a big pan of boiling salted water and turn the heat down to low. Leave the gnocchi in the water for a few minutes, it will rise to the surface when done.

For the pesto, roast the pine nuts in a pan over a medium heat until golden brown. Let cool.

Mix the pine nuts, basil, garlic and half the cheese in a blender, adding the oil gradually until the pesto is smooth.
Season with salt.

Drain the gnocchi and mix with the pesto. Serve on warm plates, sprinkling the remaining cheese over and garnishing with basil.

# Deep-fried catfish fillets with cucumber salsa

**Prep and cook time: 25 minutes**
**Cannot be frozen**
**Serves: 4**

**Ingredients:**
1 small cucumber
700 g | 1¾ lbs catfish fillet
75 g | ¾ cup plain|all purpose flour
1 tsp paprika (sweet)
1 tsp dried thyme
½ tsp ground cumin
½ tsp Cayenne pepper
1 tbsp olive oil
1 tbsp apple vinegar
1 tbsp chopped dill tips
2 tbsp orange juice
2 tbsp light soy sauce
sugar
100 g | ⅔ cup cornmeal
2 eggs
2 tsp mustard
100 ml | 7 tbsp milk
1 litre oil, for frying

**Method:**
Wash the cucumber, cut in half lengthwise and scrape out the seeds with a spoon. Finely dice the cucumber halves, mix with a little salt and leave to stand.

Wash the fish fillets, dab dry and cut into two-bite sized pieces.

Put the flour into a deep plate and season with salt and pepper.

Mix the paprika, thyme, cumin and Cayenne pepper with the cornmeal in another deep plate.

Rinse the diced cucumber in cold water in a sieve and drain thoroughly; squeeze out any excess liquid. Mix the oil, vinegar, dill and orange juice into the diced cucumber and season to taste with soy sauce, sugar and pepper.

Whisk the eggs with the mustard and milk in another deep plate.

Heat the deep-frying fat to 180°C / 375°F. Dip the fish fillets first in flour, then in egg and milk and finally in the seasoned cornmeal; deep fry in batches for 4 minutes until golden-brown and keep warm.

Serve the fish with the cucumber salsa.

# Meatballs with tomato sauce

**Prep and cook time: 30 minutes**
**Can be frozen**
**Serves: 6**

**Ingredients:**

1 large egg, beaten
25 g | ¼ cup Parmesan cheese, freshly grated
2 tbsp fresh parsley, chopped
½ tsp salt
½ tsp ground black pepper
¼ tsp ground nutmeg
400 g | 1 lb ground beef
1 slice white bread
60 ml | ¼ cup milk
2 tbsp olive oil
1 tbsp butter
75 g | ½ cup carrots, finely diced
75 g | ½ cup onion, finely chopped
2 garlic cloves, chopped
½ stalk celery, diced
250 ml | 1 cup chicken stock
2 lemons, juiced
800 g | 2 cans of chopped tomatoes

**Method:**

Mix the egg, Parmesan, parsley, salt, pepper and nutmeg together with the ground beef.

Soak bread in milk; squeeze out excess moisture and add to the meat mixture.

Heat the 1 tablespoon of olive oil with butter and stir in the carrots, onion and celery. Add a little stock from time to time to prevent them browning. Cook for 8 minutes.

When the vegetables are soft and cool, add to the ground beef mixture. Roll into little balls and put in a cool place to rest for 10 minutes.

Heat remaining olive oil to medium heat. Add meatballs and cook gently until they are golden brown, about 5 minutes each side. Add the lemon juice, garlic and chopped tomatoes, simmer for 5 minutes.

home
cooking.

# Leg of lamb with herb crust

**Prep and cook time: 3 hours 20 minutes**
**Can be frozen**
**Serves: 4 - 6**

**Ingredients:**
**8 cloves garlic, crushed**
**6 sprigs fresh marjoram**
**6 fresh bay leaves**
**1 handful fresh thyme**
**olive oil**
**1 leg of lamb (roughly 1.2 kg | 3 lbs)**
**balsamic vinegar**

**Method:**
Heat the oven to 160°C (140°C fan) 325°F, gas 3.

Place the garlic and 4 sprigs marjoram in a roasting pan.
Add 3 bay leaves and $1/3$ of the thyme sprigs.
Drizzle with olive oil.

Pick the leaves off the remaining thyme sprigs (reserving 2 to garnish), mix them with 2 tbsp olive oil and rub them into the lamb. Season the lamb with salt and ground pepper and lay on top of the garlic.

Roast the lamb gently for 3 hours. If necessary, add a little water and turn the lamb occasionally.

Drizzle balsamic vinegar over the meat and garnish with the remaining herbs before serving.

# Individual potato and bacon quiches

**Prep and cook time: 1 hour  Rising: 45 minutes**
**Cannot be frozen**
**Serves: 4**

**Ingredients:**
**For the dough:**
**200 g 1¾ cups plain|all purpose flour**
**3 g | ½ tsp yeast**
**½ tsp sugar**
**1 tsp salt**
**50 ml | 10 tsp vegetable oil**

**For the filling:**
**1 leek, thinly sliced**
**800 g | 2 lbs potatoes, thinly sliced**
**150 g | ¾ cup cream cheese**
**250 ml | 1 cup cream**
**50 g | ½ cup fresh Parmesan cheese, grated**
**3 eggs**
**nutmeg**
**60 g | ⅓ cup smoked bacon, in strips**

**To garnish:**
**4 sprigs rosemary**

**Method:**
For the dough, place the flour in a bowl and sprinkle with the yeast, sugar, salt and oil. Add 125 ml / ½ cup lukewarm water and knead to a smooth dough. Cover and let rise in a warm place for 30 minutes.

Heat the oven to 200°C (180°C fan) 400°F, gas 6.

Oil the quiche pans. Roll out the dough and line the pans. Spread the potato and leek slices on the dough.

Beat the cream cheese with the cream, Parmesan and eggs. Season with salt, ground pepper and nutmeg. Pour the mixture over the potatoes and leeks to cover them. Sprinkle with bacon strips.

Bake for 35 minutes until golden brown. Garnish with rosemary and serve.

# Creole chicken with curried rice

**Prep and cook time: 1 hour 10 minutes**
**Cannot be frozen**
**Serves: 4**

**Ingredients:**
**1 chicken, divided into 8 pieces**
**3 tbsp vegetable oil**
**$\frac{1}{2}$ tsp ground cumin**
**1 tbsp curry powder**
**3 cloves garlic, finely chopped**
**200 ml | $\frac{7}{8}$ cup chicken stock**
**1 kg | 2 lbs tomatoes; skinned and quartered**
**250 g | $\frac{1}{2}$ lb mangetout**

**For the rice:**
**300 g | 2 cups long grain rice**
**20 g | $\frac{1}{8}$ cup butter**
**1 pinch saffron**
**125 ml | $\frac{1}{2}$ cup chicken stock**
**pink peppercorns, lightly crushed**

**Method:**

Rub salt and pepper into the chicken pieces. Heat the oil in a skillet and sear the chicken pieces until browned all over. Sprinkle with cumin and curry powder and cook for 3 minutes.

Add the garlic and stock to the chicken. Stir in the tomatoes, cover and simmer gently for 30 minutes.

In a separate pan, cook the rice in boiling, lightly salted water for 10-15 minutes, making sure it does not boil dry, add a little more water if necessary.

Add the mangetout to the chicken and continue to cook for a further 10 minutes until the chicken is cooked. Season with salt and pepper.

Heat the butter in a pan, add the saffron and pour on the stock. Add $\frac{1}{3}$ of the rice and stir well until the liquid has evaporated.

Place the remaining rice in a bowl and top with the saffron rice. Sprinkle with the pink peppercorns and serve with the chicken.

# Beef burgers

**Prep and cook time: 40 minutes**
**Cannot be frozen**
**Serves: 4**

**Ingredients:**
3 tbsp olive oil
1 shallot, finely chopped
2 tbsp fresh parsley, chopped
1 tbsp fresh marjoram leaves, chopped
1 egg
1 tbsp ketchup
2 cloves garlic
400 g | 1 lb mixed ground beef
and pork
breadcrumbs
4 burger rolls
1 red onion, sliced in rings
2 tomatoes, cored and sliced
2 lettuce leaves
4 tbsp mustard

**Method:**
Heat 1 tbsp oil and fry the shallot, garlic and breadcrumbs. Add the parsley and marjoram and allow to cool slightly.

Mix it with the shallot, the egg and ketchup. Mix in the meat, until the mixture can be shaped, it shouldn't be too soft. Season generously with salt and ground pepper.

Shape into burgers, brush them with the remaining oil and fry for 2-3 minutes on each side.

Slice the rolls and lay with the cut side on the grill for 1-2 minutes until golden brown.

Spread 1 tbsp mustard on each roll and cover with the burger. Place the onion, tomato and lettuce on the burger. Top with the other half of the roll and serve.

# Snapper pie

**Prep and cook time: 1 hour 15 minutes**
**Cannot be frozen**
**Serves: 4**

**Ingredients:**
**1400 g | 1 lb snapper fillets**
**3-4 tbsp lemon juice**
**200 g | ½ lb puff pastry**
**1 onion**
**1 leek (white part only)**
**1 tbsp butter**
**1 heaped tbsp plain|all purpose flour**
**200 ml | ⅞ cup milk**
**200 ml | ⅞ cup coconut milk**
**grated zest of half a lemon**
**150 g | ⅔ cup pineapple chunks**
**melted butter, for brushing the pastry**

**Method:**

Heat the oven to 180°C (160°C fan) 375°F, gas 5.

Cut the fish into bite-sized pieces and sprinkle with half of the lemon juice.

Peel and finely chop the onion. Trim the leek and cut into thin strips. Heat the butter and sweat the onion and leek until translucent.

Dust the fish with flour and stir in the milk and coconut milk. Season with salt and white pepper and add lemon zest. Chop the pineapple and mix into the sauce.

Place the pieces of fish in a buttered baking dish and cover with the sauce. Roll out the puff pastry to fit the dish and place on top of the filling. Brush with melted butter and bake in the oven for 30-40 minutes, until golden brown.

# Shepherd's pie

**Prep and cook time: 1 hour 15 minutes**
**Can be frozen**
**Serves: 4**

**Ingredients:**
**300 g | ⅔ lb potatoes, peeled**
**2 tbsp oil**
**400 g | 1 lb ground lamb**
**2 onions, finely chopped**
**1 tsp tomato paste**
**40 ml | 8 tsp hot milk**
**nutmeg**
**50 g | ½ cup Cheddar cheese, grated**

**Method:**

Heat the oven to 200°C (180°C fan) 400°F, gas 6.

Cook the potatoes in boiling salted water for 20 minutes or until tender.

Heat the oil and fry the onions until translucent, then add the meat and cook for about 10 minutes. Add tomato paste and season with salt and pepper.

Drain and mash the potatoes. Stir in the hot milk and season with salt, pepper and nutmeg.

Butter 4 (small) oven-proof bowls or soufflé dishes 250 ml / 1 cup capacity, or one large oven-proof dish.

Spoon the meat into the bowls, top with the mashed potato and sprinkle with cheese. Bake on the middle shelf for 20 minutes.

# Rosemary roasted chicken

**Prep and cook time: 1 hour 30 minutes**
**Cannot be frozen**
**Serves: 4 - 6**

**Ingredients:**
**For the stuffing:**
**70 ml | 14 tsp milk**
**2 tbsp coarse wheat bran**
**1 tbsp butter**
**50 g | 1/3 cup leek (white part only), finely chopped**
**1 tbsp chopped parsley**
**3 tsp fresh rosemary, chopped**
**1 egg**
**1 large chicken**
**1 tbsp butter**

**Method:**

Boil the milk, pour it over the wheat bran and let soak, covered.

Heat the butter and fry the leek until golden brown. Stir in the parsley. Add the milk and wheat bran and bring to a boil quickly. Let the stuffing cool slightly and mix in 1 tsp rosemary, 1/2 tsp salt, 1 pinch pepper and the egg.

Heat the oven to 220°C (200°C fan) 425°F, gas 7.

Spoon the stuffing into the cavity of the chicken. Rub the remaining rosemary with a little salt and pepper into the skin.

Place the chicken on a wire rack in a roasting pan. Dot the chicken with small pieces of butter and roast for 25 minutes. Gently spoon the meat juices over chicken and then roast for a further 30-35 minutes until done. Allow the meat to rest before it is served for 5-10 minutes.

# Meatballs with tomatoes and olives

**Prep and cook time: 40 minutes**
**Can be frozen**
**Serves: 4**

**Ingredients:**
**For the tomato sauce:**
800 g | 3¹/₂ cups tomatoes, chopped
2 shallots, finely chopped
2 cloves garlic, crushed
3 tbsp olive oil
1 tbsp tomato puree
2 sprigs thyme
10 g | ¹/₂ cup basil leaves,
finely chopped
50 g | ¹/₂ cup green olives, pitted

**For the meatballs:**
1 shallot, finely chopped
1 tbsp butter
2 stale bread rolls
a little milk, for soaking
500 g | 1¹/₄ lbs ground lamb
1 egg
2 tbsp chopped parsley
¹/₂ tsp salt
freshly ground pepper
4 tbsp olive oil

**Method:**

For the tomato sauce, heat the olive oil in a skillet and gently cook the shallots and garlic. Add the tomato puree and cook for a further 3-4 minutes. Add the tomatoes and one sprig of thyme and simmer for 20 minutes, stirring occasionally, until quite thick.

Add the basil leaves and the rest of the thyme leaves, season with salt and pepper and stir in the olives.

For the meatballs, cook the shallots in butter until translucent. Soak the bread rolls in milk, then squeeze out and add to the ground lamb with the shallots and the egg.

Add the parsley, season with salt and pepper and mix well. With wet hands form into small balls. Heat the oil in a clean skillet and fry the meatballs on all sides for about 6 minutes until golden brown.

Serve the meatballs in the tomato sauce.

# Bacon-wrapped meatloaf with potatoes

**Prep and cook time: 1 hour 35 minutes**
**Cannot be frozen**
**Serves: 4**

**Ingredients:**
1 tbsp butter
1 onion, finely chopped
1 clove garlic, finely chopped
250 g | ½ lb celery stalk, finely chopped, reserve the leaves for decoration
2 slices dried bread, crusts cut off (or a day-old bread roll)
500 g | 1 lb ground pork or beef, or a mix of both
1 egg
1 tsp mustard
2 tbsp vegetable oil
150 g | 6 slices bacon
800 g | 2 lbs small or new potatoes, scrubbed
2 lemons, squeeze the juice of one lemon, slice the other
1 sprig rosemary, leaves chopped
2 sprigs thyme, leaves chopped

**Method:**
Heat the oven to 180°C (160°C fan) 375°F, gas 5.

Heat the butter in a pan and fry the onion, garlic and celery stalk for 2-4 minutes over low to medium heat. Season with salt and pepper.

Soften the bread in a little water. Place the meat with the egg, mustard and the cooked vegetables in a bowl. Squeeze the excess water from the bread and add. Mix everything thoroughly and season generously with salt and pepper.

Oil a large roasting pan with 1 tbsp oil. Shape the meat to a loaf shape in the pan and wrap the bacon slices around it.

Place the potatoes in a bowl with the remaining 1 tbsp oil. Add the rosemary, thyme, lemon juice and 1 small tbsp salt and mix well. Place the potatoes around the meat loaf.

Bake the meatloaf and potatoes on the middle shelf for 55-60 minutes, until they are done. Turn the potatoes occasionally during the cooking time.

Garnish the meatloaf and potatoes with the celery leaves and decorate the potatoes with lemon slices.

# Sausage and mash with bacon and blueberry sauce

**Prep and cook time: 45 minutes**
**Cannot be frozen**
**Serves: 4**

**Ingredients:**
**For the mashed potatoes:**
**400 g | 14 oz floury potatoes, peeled and roughly chopped**
**200 g | 7 oz savoy leaves, chopped**
**100 ml | 3½ fl oz | 7 tbsp milk**
**15 g | ½ oz softened butter**
**freshly ground nutmeg, for seasoning**

**For the sauce:**
**1 chilli pepper, finely chopped**
**1 tbsp vegetable oil**
**100 ml | 3 ½ fl oz | 7 tbsp red wine**
**100 ml | 3 ½ fl oz | 7 tbsp redcurrant juice**
**100 g | 3 ½ oz blueberries**
**100 g | 3 ½ oz redcurrants**

**In addition:**
**12 small pork sausages**
**60 g | 2 oz cubed bacon**
**2 tbsp vegetable oil**

**Method:**

Cook the potatoes in salted, boiling water for 30 minutes until they can be easily pierced with a knife.

Blanch the cabbage for 5 minutes in salted water. Drain.

Drain the potatoes. Run the potatoes through a potato ricer while still hot.

Heat the milk, cream and butter in a saucepan. Gradually stir the milk mixture into the mashed potatoes with a spoon.

Stir in the cabbage. Season to taste with salt, pepper and the freshly ground nutmeg. Keep warm over a hot water bath.

Sauté the chilli pepper in hot oil.

Pour in the red wine and the juice. Simmer for 5 minutes.

While waiting, rinse the redcurrants and blueberries and then add them to the sauce. Simmer gently for 5 minutes.

Fry the sausages with the bacon in hot oil until golden brown on all sides (6 minutes). Arrange on plates along with the mashed potatoes. Spoon the sauce around the sides dividing it equally among the plates.

# Braised lamb shank

**Prep and cook time: 2 hours 30 minutes**
**Can be frozen**
**Serves: 4**

**Ingredients:**
1 large onion, peeled and diced
1 carrot, peeled and diced
120 g | 1 cup celeriac|celery root,
peeled and diced
1 small fennel bulb, trimmed and diced
1 small leek, trimmed and chopped
2 tbsp oil
4 lamb shanks
1 tbsp icing|confectioners' sugar
100 ml | 7 tbsp red port
250 ml | 1 cup strong red wine
1 tbsp tomato paste
400 ml | 1 ⅔ cups lamb stock
4 fresh bay leaves
2 tsp cornflour|cornstarch
1 garlic clove, crushed
1 tsp fresh ginger, peeled
and finely chopped
1 strip of lemon peel
6 sprigs thyme

**Method:**
Heat the oven to 150°C (130°C fan) 300°F, gas 2.

Heat the oil in an ovenproof stew pot and brown the lamb shanks on all sides over a medium heat. Take out of the pot and pour off the frying fat.

Put the icing/confectioners' sugar into the pot, caramelise lightly and deglaze with the port and ⅓ of the red wine.
Stir in the tomato paste and simmer the sauce until it has the consistency of syrup.

Add the rest of the red wine in 2 portions, simmering to reduce slightly between each addition. Add the chopped onions, carrots, celeriac/celery root, fennel and stock to the sauce.

Add the lamb shanks, cover and cook for 2½ hours until the meat is tender, turning the shanks frequently during cooking. After 2 hours add the diced leek and bay leaves.

Take out the lamb shanks, pour the sauce through a sieve and reserve the vegetables and bay leaves. Transfer the sauce to a pan and simmer to reduce slightly. Mix the cornflour/cornstarch with a little cold water, stir into the sauce and simmer gently for 1-2 minutes.

Remove the pan from the heat, add the garlic, ginger, lemon peel and thyme. Allow to infuse for a few minutes, then sieve again. Season with salt and pepper. Return the sauce to pan with the lamb shanks and vegetables and reheat gently.

# Steak and ale pie

**Prep and cook time: 1 hour 15 minutes  Chilling time: 2 hours**
**Can be frozen**
**Serves: 6**

**Ingredients:**
**For the short crust pastry:**
**500 g | 4 cups plain|all purpose flour**
**250 g | 1 cup butter**
**2 eggs**

**For the filling:**
**800 g | 2 lb beef steaks, chopped into bite sized pieces**
**2 tbsp vegetable oil**
**3 stems thyme, leaves picked**
**2-3 tbsp plain|all purpose flour**
**150 ml | ²/₃ cup ale**
**100 g | ³/₄ cup mushrooms, finely sliced**

**Also needed:**
**1 egg yolk, beaten**

**Method:**

For the dough, sift the flour into a bowl and make a well in the middle. Dot pieces of the butter, salt, eggs and 2 tbsp water into the well. Knead quickly to form a dough. Shape the dough into a ball, wrap in cling film and chill in the fridge for 2 hours.

Heat the oven to 200°C (180°C fan) 400°F, gas 6.

Season the beef with salt and pepper. Heat the oil in a pan and fry the meat until brown all over. Add the thyme leaves.

Sprinkle the flour over the meat and pour on the ale. Bring to a boil and season with salt and pepper, and allow it to cool. The sauce should be fairly thick. Mix in the mushrooms.

Roll out the pastry and cut out two circles. One should be large enough to cover the base of the pie dish. Line the pie dish with the larger circle and spoon on the meat and sauce.
Cover with a pastry lid. Press the edges down firmly.
The edges may be decorated.

Brush the pie with beaten egg yolk and bake for 45 minutes until golden brown.

# Boulangere potatoes with parsnips

**Prep and cook time: 1 hour**
**Cannot be frozen**
**Serves: 4**

**Ingredients:**
50 g | ½ cup butter
500 g | 1¼ lb waxy potatoes,
thinly sliced
300 g | ¾ lbs parsnips, thinly sliced
100 ml | 7 tbsp white wine
400 ml | 1⅔ cups chicken stock

**Method:**
Heat the oven to 180°C (160°C fan) 375°F, gas 5.

Butter an ovenproof dish and arrange the potatoes and parsnips in layers in the dish, seasoning thoroughly with salt and ground pepper.

Pour on the wine and stock to just cover the potatoes and parsnips. Dot with small pieces of butter.

Bake for 35 minutes until golden brown.

# Fried pork chop with herbs and herb cream sauce

**Prep and cook time: 40 minutes**
**Cannot be frozen**
**Serves: 4**

**Ingredients:**
**For the herb cream sauce:**
**2 tbsp butter**
**1 onion, chopped**
**2 tbsp plain|all purpose flour**
**300 ml | 1⅓ cups meat stock**
**2 tbsp fresh chopped herbs (parsley, chervil, rosemary and thyme)**
**100 ml | 7 tbsp crème fraiche**
**nutmeg**
**lemon juice**

**For the meat:**
**4 pork chops**
**1 tsp caraway, crushed**
**2 tbsp fresh chopped herbs (rosemary, thyme, marjoram)**
**2 tbsp sunflower oil**

**Method:**

For the herb cream sauce, heat the butter in a pan and fry the onion gently until transparent. Stir in the flour and fry briefly. Pour in the stock and boil over a low heat for 5 minutes, continuing to stir.

Add the herbs to the sauce. Stir in the crème fraiche and puree the sauce. Season the pan with salt, ground pepper, nutmeg and lemon juice.

Season the pork chops with salt, pepper and caraway and sprinkle with the herbs. Heat the sunflower oil in a skillet and fry the chops gently for 3-4 minutes on each side.
Serve with the sauce.

# Beef wellington

**Prep and cook time: 1 hour 40 minutes**
**Cannot be frozen**
**Serves: 4**

**Ingredients:**
2 tbsp butter
1 shallot, finely chopped
250 g | 2 cups mushrooms, finely chopped
40 ml | 8 tsp Madeira
3 tbsp cream
2 tbsp parsley, finely chopped
800 g | 2 lb fillet of beef
2 tbsp vegetable oil
400 g | 1 lb puff pastry
100 g | ¼ lb goose liver pâté
2 egg yolks

**Method:**

Heat the butter and fry the chopped shallot until soft. Add the mushrooms and fry slowly until the liquid has evaporated.

Pour in the Madeira, let boil then add the cream and cook over a high heat to reduce. Season with salt and ground pepper, mix in the parsley and let cool.

Rub salt and ground pepper into the beef. Heat the oil in a skillet and fry the beef on all sides over a high heat. Take out and let rest.

Heat the oven to 220°C (200°C fan) 425°F, gas 7.

Roll out the pastry so the beef can be wrapped in it. Cut off a few thin strips for decoration.

Place ¼ of the mushroom mixture on the pastry. Spread one side of the beef with some of the liver pâté and lay it with this side down on the mushrooms. Spread the remaining pâté on the meat, then the remaining mushroom mixture.

Fold the pastry over the meat. Wrap up tightly and press the edges and sides together firmly. Lay with the pastry join underneath on a cookie sheet lined with baking parchment. Brush with beaten egg yolk and bake for 40 minutes.

Cut in slices to serve.

# Moussaka

**Prep and cook time: 1 hour 50 minutes**
**Can be frozen**
**Serves: 4**

**Ingredients:**
5 tbsp olive oil
1 onion, chopped
2 cloves garlic, chopped
400 g | 1 lb mixed pork and
beef, ground
240 g | 2½ cups canned
tomatoes, chopped
1 tsp dried oregano
500 g | 1¼ lbs aubergine|eggplant,
thinly sliced lengthways
600 g | 1½ lbs potatoes, peeled,
thinly sliced
200 g | 1½ cups feta cheese
50 g | ¼ cup butter
40 g | ¼ cup plain|all purpose flour
400 ml | 1⅔ cups milk

**Method:**
Heat the oven to 220°C (200°C fan) 425°F, gas 7.

Heat 1 tbsp olive oil in a wide pan. Fry the onion and garlic for 2 minutes over a low to medium heat until soft. Add the meat, turn up the heat and stir continuously, until the meat is browned.

Stir in the tomatoes and the oregano. Season with salt and pepper. Simmer for 20 minutes over a low to medium heat until reduced.

Oil a cookie sheet, lay the aubergine/eggplant slices on the sheet and brush with 1 tbsp oil. Bake on the middle shelf for 8 minutes until slightly browned.

Take out the aubergine/eggplant and turn the oven down to 180°C (160°C fan) 375°F, gas 5. Oil an oven-proof dish (20 x 25 cm / 8 x 10").

Lay one third of the potato slices in the dish. Spread half the meat sauce and half the aubergine/eggplant over the potato. Crumble in ¼ of the feta cheese. Repeat these layers, ending with a layer of potato. Season lightly with salt and pepper.

Melt the butter in a small pan and fry the flour quickly. Gradually stir in the milk. Simmer the sauce over a low heat for 5-8 minutes until thickened. Chop the remaining feta cheese and add it to the sauce. Puree with a hand-held mixer.

Season the cheese sauce with salt and pepper and pour over the moussaka. Bake the moussaka on the middle shelf for 55-60 minutes until golden brown.

# Boeuf bourguignon

**Prep and cook time: 3 hours 40 minutes**
**Can be frozen**
**Serves: 4**

**Ingredients:**
2 tbsp olive oil
100 g | ½ cup fatty bacon,
cut into strips
800 g | 2 lbs beef, chopped into
large chunks
2 tbsp tomato paste
500 ml | 2 cups red wine
125 ml | ½ cup meat stock
20 ml | 4 tsp cognac
500 g | 1 ¼ lbs small turnips, or carrots
200 g | ¼ lb onions, chopped
into wedges
3 cloves garlic, quartered
3 sprigs thyme
2 bay leaves
20 g ⅛ cup butter
2 tbsp plain|all purpose flour

**Method:**
Heat the oven to 160°C (140°C fan) 325°F, gas 3.

Heat the olive oil in a large skillet. Fry the bacon and remove.

Fry the beef in the bacon fat until browned on all sides. Stir in the tomato paste and pour in the wine, stock and cognac.

Add the bacon, turnips, onion, garlic, thyme and bay leaves. Season lightly with salt and ground pepper. Transfer to an oven-proof dish, cover and cook in the oven for 3 hours, stirring occasionally.

Knead the butter with the flour and stir into the casserole. Continue to cook for a further 10 minutes, uncovered.

Season with salt and ground pepper and garnish with marjoram to serve.

# Lancashire hotpot

**Prep and cook time: 1 hour 50 minutes**
**Cannot be frozen**
**Serves: 4**

**Ingredients:**
500 g | 1¼ lbs lamb, neck fillet
600 g | 1½ lbs waxy potatoes
20 g | 2 tbsp butter
1 onion
2 carrots
1 medium celeriac|celery root
750 ml | 3 cups lamb stock
2 tbsp marjoram, chopped

**Method:**
Heat the oven to 200°C (180°C fan) 400°F, gas 6.

Wash the meat, pat dry and cut into smallish cubes.

Peel the potatoes and slice thinly. Peel and finely dice the other vegetables.

Butter a casserole dish and put all the ingredients into it in layers, beginning with a layer of potatoes, then vegetables and then meat. Season with salt, pepper and marjoram between layers. Finish with a neat layer of potatoes and season again.

Pour the stock over, cover and simmer for 90 minutes. Shortly before the end of cooking time remove the lid to brown the potatoes.

# Chilli con carne with sour cream

**Prep and cook time: 1 hour**
**Can be frozen**
**Serves: 4**

**Ingredients:**
2 tbsp olive oil
1 onion, finely chopped
2 cloves garlic, finely chopped
500 g | 1¼ pound ground beef
2 red chillies, finely chopped
1 tbsp tomato paste
1 red bell pepper, finely chopped
1 tbsp ground paprika, hot
200 ml | ⅞ cup meat stock
300 g | 12oz | 1 ⅓ cups canned
chopped tomatoes
300 g | 4 cups canned kidney
beans, drained

**To garnish:**
chives, chopped
4 tbsp sour cream

**Method:**
Heat the oil in a skillet and fry the onion and garlic. Add the beef and chilli and fry over a high heat for 5 minutes.

Add the tomato paste and fry briefly with the other ingredients. Stir in the chopped bell pepper and ground paprika. Pour on the stock and the tomatoes.

Simmer gently for 30 minutes, stirring occasionally. Add a little more stock if necessary. Add the beans and simmer for a further 10 minutes until done.

Season with salt and pepper. Serve with a spoonful of sour cream on each and garnish with chives.

# Roast pork with crackling and baked apples

**Prep and cook time: 1 hour 30 minutes**
**Cannot be frozen**
**Serves: 4**

**Ingredients:**

1.5 kg | 3 lbs saddle or rolled
loin of pork, boned and tied
2 cloves garlic
2 onions, chopped
2 tbsp vegetable oil
1 bay leaf
8 small apples, whole, cored

**Method:**

Heat the oven to 200°C (180°C fan) 400°F, gas 6.

Lay on a wire rack in a roasting pan with the skin on top. Score the skin with a knife and pour boiling water over the skin, this will help to create fantastic crackling. Drain the water from the pan, pat the pork dry. Season the saddle of pork generously with salt and pepper.

Place the oil in a roasting pan, add the onions and garlic, coat with oil and place the rack with the pork on top. Roast for 20 minutes.

Add 250 ml / 1 cup water and the bay leaf. Roast for a further 30 minutes, adding a little more water if necessary.

Place the apples on the rack around the pork. Increase the oven temperature to 240°C. Roast for a further 20 minutes until the pork crackling is crisp and the apples are cooked.

Skim the fat off the pan juices, sieve and season with salt and pepper. Allow the meat to rest once it is removed from the oven for 10 minutes before serving.

# Lamb vindaloo

**Prep and cook time: 2 hours  Marinating time: 8 hours**
**Can be frozen**
**Serves: 4**

**Ingredients:**
**Ingredients:**
**800 g | 2 lbs lamb, from the shoulder**
**2 onions, finely chopped**
**3 cloves garlic, crushed**
**1 tsp fresh ginger, peeled and grated**
**1-2 tsp cumin seeds**
**2 tsp black mustard seeds**
**1 cinnamon stick**
**2 cloves**
**2 dried chillies**
**2 tsp turmeric**
**6 tbsp oil**
**2 tbsp mild vinegar**
**ground coriander, to season**
**brown sugar, to season**

**Serve with:**
**250 g | 1¼ cups rice**
**1 pinch saffron**
**40 g | ⅓ cup cashew nuts**
**coriander|cilantro**

**Method:**

Cut the lamb into 2 cm / ¾" cubes and place in a bowl.

Heat a large dry skillet and toast cumin, mustard seeds, cinnamon, cloves, chillies and turmeric 1-2 minutes. Remove the spices from the pan, place in a mortar and grind.

Heat 2 tbsp of oil in the skillet and fry the onion mixture for 5 minutes. Add the spices, cook for 2 minutes then add the vinegar and stir until it bubbles.

Puree the mixture to a fine paste. Mix together with the meat and marinate for at least 8 hours or leave to marinate overnight.

Heat the remaining oil in a skillet. Remove the meat from the marinade and fry on all sides. Add 400 ml / 1½ cups water. Stir in the remaining marinade and simmer at a low temperature for about 1 hour. Add a little water if necessary.

Cook the rice according to the instructions on the packet, adding the saffron to the cooking water. Drain if necessary and set aside. Toast the cashew nuts in a pan for 1-2 minutes until golden brown.

Season the lamb with ground coriander, sugar, salt and ground pepper. Divide between bowls, garnish with fresh coriander/cilantro leaves and serve with rice and cashew nuts.

# Fish and chips

**Prep and cook time: 45 minutes**
**Cannot be frozen**
**Serves: 4**

**Ingredients:**
1500 ml | 6 cups oil, for deep-frying
1 kg | 2¼ lbs potatoes, peeled
and cut into chips
800 g | 2 lbs fish fillet of your choice
2 tbsp lemon juice
3-4 tbsp plain|all purpose flour
2 eggs
100 g | 1½ cups breadcrumbs,
for coating

**Method:**
Prepare the deep-fryer and heat the oil to 170°C / 350°F - or heat the oil in a large saucepan. The oil is hot enough when small bubbles appear on a wooden spoon handle dipped into the oil.

Fry the potato chips in batches for 5 minutes until they are soft but have not changed colour. Take out and drain on paper towels.

Turn up the temperature to 190°C / 375°F and fry the potatoes again in batches for 2 minutes until brown and crispy.
Take out and drain thoroughly; keep warm.

Season the fish with salt and pepper and drizzle with lemon juice. Beat the egg and place the flour and breadcrumbs on plates.

Turn the fish in the flour, dip it into the egg and then coat it in the breadcrumbs. Fry in the deep-fryer (or saucepan) at 170°C / 350°F in batches for 4-5 minutes until golden brown.

Sprinkle the chips with salt and serve with the fish.

rice &
pasta.

# Gnocchi with Gorgonzola sauce and basil

**Prep and cook time: 1 hour 20 minutes**
**Can be frozen**
**Serves: 4**

**Ingredients:**
**500 g | 1 ¼ lb floury potatoes**
**150 g | 1¼ cups plain|all purpose flour**
**50 g | 2oz | ⅓ cup semolina|cream of wheat**
**1 egg**
**1 egg yolk**
**nutmeg**

**For the sauce:**
**200 g | 2 cups Gorgonzola cheese, crumbled**
**150 ml | ⅔ cup cream**
**200 ml | ⅞ cup vegetable stock**

**To garnish:**
**basil leaves**
**2 tbsp chives, chopped**

**Method:**

Boil the peeled and chopped potatoes in salted water for 20 minutes until done. Mash the drained potatoes and allow to cool.

Add the flour, semolina/cream of wheat, egg and egg yolk to the mashed potato. Mix well and season with salt and nutmeg. Adjust the quantity of flour so the dough is not too sticky and is easy to shape.

For the sauce, stir the Gorgonzola, cream and stock in a pan over a medium heat. Season with salt and pepper and keep warm over a low heat.

Roll out the gnocchi dough on a floured surface to rolls roughly 2 cm / 1" thick. Cut into small gnocchi. The gnocchi may be decorated with patterns, using a fork.

Place the gnocchi in a pan of simmering salted water and cook until they rise to the surface, this will take only a few minutes. Remove with a slotted spoon and drain.

Stir the gnocchi into the sauce and serve, sprinkled with basil and chives.

# Macaroni and cheese

**Prep and cook time: 1 hour 15 minutes**
**Can be frozen**
**Serves: 6 - 8**

**Ingredients:**
**6 slices white bread, torn**
**into rough pieces**
**100 g | 1/2 cup butter**
**400 g | 1 lb elbow macaroni**
**40 g | 1/3 cup plain|all purpose flour**
**1 1/2 tsp powdered mustard**
**1/4 tsp Cayenne pepper**
**1250 ml | 5 cups milk**
**200 g | 2 cups Monterey Jack**
**(or Gouda) cheese, grated**
**200 g | 2 cups Cheddar cheese, grated**
**1 tsp salt**

**Method:**
Pulse the bread and 3 tbsp of the butter in food processor until fine crumbs are formed. Set aside.

Bring a pan of water to a boil with 1 tbsp salt. Add the macaroni and cook until it is tender, drain the macaroni and set aside.

Heat the remaining butter in a pan over medium-high heat until foaming. Add the flour, mustard, and Cayenne and stir for 2 minutes. Gradually whisk in milk, bring the mixture to the boil then reduce the heat and simmer, whisking occasionally, until the sauce has thickened to the consistency of heavy cream.

Remove the pan from the heat, whisk in the cheese and 1 teaspoon salt until cheeses are fully melted. Add the macaroni and cook for a further 2 minutes.

Transfer the mixture to an oven proof dish 30 cm x 22 cm (13" x 9") and sprinkle evenly with bread crumbs and any extra cheese.

Grill until crumbs are deep, golden brown (3-5 minutes), rotating the pan if necessary for even browning.
Allow it to cool for 5 minutes and serve.

# Cannelloni filled with salmon and spinach

**Prep and cook time: 1 hour**
**Cannot be frozen**
**Serves: 4**

**Ingredients:**
250 g | ½ lb lasagne sheets,
or ready prepared cannelloni tubes
3 tbsp butter
1 onion, finely chopped
1 clove garlic, crushed
250 g | ½ lb spinach
2 tbsp crème fraiche
nutmeg, freshly grated
600 g | 1½ lbs salmon fillet,
sliced into 12 long pieces
2 tbsp plain|all purpose flour
400 ml | 1⅔ cups milk
100 g | 1 cup Parmesan cheese, grated

**Method:**
Bring plenty of salted water to the boil. Cook the pasta sheets in the water until they begin to soften and bend, remove immediately. Dip into cold water and lay on a kitchen towel to dry. Skip this step if you have cannelloni tubes.

Heat 1 tbsp butter in a pan and fry the onion and garlic over a medium heat until soft. Add the spinach and cook until it wilts. Stir in the crème fraiche and season with salt, ground pepper and nutmeg.

Butter an ovenproof dish. Lay some spinach and a salmon strip on each pasta sheet and roll up. Lay in the dish with the join underneath. Alternatively, fill the cannelloni tubes with the spinach and salmon.

Heat the oven to 200°C (180°C fan) 400°F, gas 6.

Melt the remaining butter. Stir in the flour and fry until golden brown, then gradually stir in the milk with a balloon whisk. Bring to the boil briefly, stirring continuously. Season with salt, ground pepper and nutmeg.

Pour the sauce over the pasta rolls and sprinkle with cheese. Bake for 20-25 minutes until the salmon is done and the pasta rolls are lightly browned.

# Lasagne al forno

**Prep and cook time: 1 hour 30 minutes**
**Can be frozen**
**Serves: 4**

**Ingredients:**
**For the mince sauce:**
**1 onion**
**2 cloves garlic**
**2 tsp olive oil**
**60 g | ⅔ cup button mushrooms**
**400 g | 1 lb ground beef**
**600 g | 3 cups tomatoes, chopped**
**2 tsp mixed herbs**
**(thyme, sage, rosemary, oregano)**

**For the béchamel sauce:**
**2 tbsp butter**
**1½ tbsp flour**
**400 ml | 1⅔ cups milk**
**nutmeg**
**200 g | ½ lb lasagne riccia sheets**
**100 g | 1 cup grated Pecorino**

**Method:**

Heat the oven to 180°C (160°C fan) 375°F, gas 5.

Peel and finely chop the onion and garlic. Heat the oil and sweat the onion and garlic until translucent.

Add the mushrooms and meat and break up the mince to brown right through. Add the chopped tomatoes and simmer for 10 minutes. Season with salt, pepper and herbs.

For the béchamel, melt the butter in a pan, stir in the flour and cook briefly. Whisk in the milk, season with salt, pepper and nutmeg and cook gently over a low heat for 15 minutes, stirring occasionally.

Grease a baking dish 30 cm x 20 cm / 12" x 8" and fill with alternate layers of mince, béchamel sauce and lasagne, finishing with béchamel sauce and cheese.

Bake the lasagne in the preheated oven for 40-45 minutes until lightly browned on top.

# Whole-wheat spaghetti with chanterelle mushrooms and Parmesan

**Prep and cook time: 20 minutes**
**Cannot be frozen**
**Serves: 4**

**Ingredients:**
**500 g | 1 ¼ lb whole-wheat spaghetti**
**4 tbsp olive oil**
**2 shallots, chopped**
**2 cloves garlic, chopped**
**300 g | 2 cups chanterelles, chopped if large**
**300 g | 2 cups oyster mushrooms, chopped if large**
**20 g | 1 cup basil, chopped leaves**
**50 g | ½ cup Parmesan cheese, shavings**
**50 ml single cream**

**Method:**

Cook the spaghetti in plenty of salted water for 7-8 minutes until al dente. Drain in a sieve; dip into cold water and drain.

Heat the oil in a skillet and fry the shallots and garlic. Add the mushrooms and fry briefly but over a high heat. Season with salt, ground pepper and basil. Remove the pan from the heat and add the cream, gently stirring to warm.

Add the drained spaghetti to the pan and coat the spaghetti in the sauce. Stir until the pasta is heated through, then season if needed.

Garnish with Parmesan shavings and serve.

# Small pasta bakes with Taleggio cheese and prosciutto

**Prep and cook time: 1 hour**
**Can be frozen**
**Serves: 4 as a starter**

**Ingredients:**
150 g | 1 cup ditalini pasta,
or other small pasta
4 slices prosciutto
1 shallot
30 g | 2 tbsp butter
250 ml | 1 cup crème fraiche
200 g | ½ lb Taleggio cheese,
or other strong cheese
8 sprigs thyme
2 eggs
40 g | 1 cup breadcrumbs

**Method:**
Heat the oven to 180°C (160°C fan) 375°F, gas 5.

Cook the pasta in boiling, salted water for 7-8 minutes until al dente, then refresh in cold water and drain well.

Butter 4 small moulds and line with baking parchment, so that the paper is 1 inch (2 cm) taller than the moulds.

Cut the prosciutto into strips. Peel and finely chop the shallot. Cook the shallot in 1 ½ tbsp butter until soft, then add the prosciutto and remove from the heat.

Place half of the pasta in the bottom of the moulds. Put the prosciutto - shallot mix on top, followed by the rest of the pasta. Fill so that the pasta is as tall as the baking parchment.

Puree the crème fraiche and the Taleggio cheese in a blender. Pull the thyme leaves off the stem and chop. Save 4 sprigs for the garnish. Stir the chopped thyme and eggs into the crème fraiche mix. Season with salt and pepper, then pour over the pasta.

Sprinkle breadcrumbs on top of the pasta and add a few knobs of butter. Bake in the oven on the middle shelf for 30 minutes. Garnish with the sprigs of thyme and serve immediately.

# Penne all'arrabbiata – penne with chilli, bacon and mushrooms

**Prep and cook time: 30 minutes**
**Cannot be frozen**
**Serves: 4**

**Ingredients:**
**2 slices bacon, diced**
**2 cloves garlic**
**1 onion**
**1 red chilli pepper**
**4 large mushrooms**
**2 tbsp. olive oil**
**300 g | 1½ cups tomatoes, chopped**
**400 g | 1 lb penne pasta**
**2 tbsp grated Parmesan cheese**
**4 sprigs basil**

**Method:**
Fry the bacon in a dry skillet until crisp. Remove and put aside. Peel and finely chop the garlic and the onion. Wash the chilli pepper, cut in half lengthways, de-seed, then cut into fine strips.

Clean the mushrooms and cut into slices. Heat the oil in a saucepan. Sauté the onion, garlic and chilli. Add the drained tomatoes and season with salt and pepper. Cover with a lid and simmer gently for 15 minutes.

Add the mushrooms 5 minutes before the end of cooking time. Now stir in the bacon and season to taste with salt and pepper.

Cook the pasta in boiling, salted water according to the instructions on the packet until al dente. Drain, the toss in the sauce. Serve with a little grated Parmesan cheese and garnish with a few basil leaves.

# Lasagne alla cremonese – lasagne with Gorgonzola, rocket and pine nuts

**Prep and cook time: 1 hour 20 minutes**
**Can be frozen**
**Serves: 4**

**Ingredients:**
100 g | ¼ lb rocket|arugula
2 shallots
40 g | 3 tbsp butter
50 g | ⅓ cup flour
700 ml | 3 cups milk
400 ml | 1⅔ cups vegetable stock
Salt & freshly ground pepper
1 tbsp lemon juice
nutmeg
200 g | 2 cups Gorgonzola
100 g | 3 tbsp pine nuts
200 g | ½ lb lasagne sheets

**Method:**
Heat the oven to 180°C (160°C gas) 375°F, gas 5

Wash the rocket/arugula, drain well and remove any hard stalks. Peel the shallots and cut into rings.

For the sauce heat the butter in a pan until it foams, then add the shallot rings and cook until translucent. Stir in the flour and cook without browning, then stir in the vegetable stock and milk and bring to the boil, stirring constantly. Simmer for about 5 minutes, then remove from the heat, cover and leave to stand for 10 minutes. Season with salt and pepper and add lemon juice and nutmeg to taste.

Spread a sauce in a baking dish 20 cm x 20 cm / 8" x 8", sprinkle with a little crumbled Gorgonzola, some rocket/arugula and a few pine nuts and cover with lasagne sheets. Continue in this way, adding the ingredients in layers (3 to 4 layers) until all the ingredients are used up. The final layer should consist of béchamel sauce, arugula, pine nuts and a little Gorgonzola.

Bake in the preheated oven for 35-40 minutes. If the lasagne appears too dry, add a little stock.

# Spaghetti bolognese

**Prep and cook time: 1 hour**
**Can be frozen**
**Serves: 4**

**Ingredients:**
**4 tbsp olive oil**
**1 onion, chopped**
**2 cloves garlic, crushed**
**8 slices smoked bacon**
**1 carrot, chopped**
**1 stalk celery, chopped**
**250 g | ¾ lb mixed pork**
**and beef, ground**
**1 tbsp tomato paste**
**100 ml | 7 tbsp red wine**
**125 ml | ½ cup strong meat stock**
**200 g | 2 cups tomatoes, chopped**
**400 g | 1 lb spaghetti**

**Method:**
Heat the oil in a pan and fry the onion, garlic and bacon. Add the vegetables and fry briefly.

Add the meat, a little at a time, and fry over a high heat for a few minutes until browned. Add the tomato paste and pour in the wine and stock. Season with salt and pepper and stir in the tomatoes.

Simmer on a low heat for 30 minutes, stirring occasionally. Add a little more stock if necessary.

Cook the spaghetti until al dente according to the package instructions.

Check the seasoning of the sauce. Drain the pasta and place in bowls. Spoon the sauce over and garnish with basil before serving.

# Cannelloni with tomato sauce and thyme

**Prep and cook time: 1 hour**
**Can be frozen**
**Serves: 4**

**Ingredients:**
**600 g | 1½ lbs spinach**
**1 onion**
**1 clove garlic**
**1 tbsp oil**
**250 g | ½ lb mozzarella**
**1 tbsp chopped basil**
**1 tbsp chopped parsley**
**250 g | 1 cup cream cheese, low fat**
**nutmeg**
**12 cannelloni tubes**
**500 g | 2 cups tomatoes, chopped**
**4 tbsp Parmesan cheese, grated**
**2 tsp fresh thyme**

**Method:**

Heat the oven to 200°C (180°C fan) 400°F, gas 6.

Wash and sort the spinach, put into a pan with a little boiling, salted water and cook until it wilts. Then drain, refresh in cold water, drain well, squeeze out and chop.

Peel and dice the onion and garlic. Heat the oil and sweat the onion and garlic until soft. Add the spinach, season with salt, pepper and sweat over a medium heat for a few minutes, stirring. Let cool.

Drain and finely dice the mozzarella. Mix the herbs, cream cheese and mozzarella with the spinach and season with salt, pepper and nutmeg.

Fill the cannelloni with the mixture. Put half of the chopped tomatoes into a greased baking dish and stir in 5 tbsp water. Lay the filled cannelloni on top and pour the rest of the tomatoes over them. Add 1 tsp thyme, season with salt and pepper.

Bake for 25 minutes. Then sprinkle with Parmesan and remaining thyme and bake for a further 10-15 minutes.

# Spaghetti carbonara

**Prep and cook time: 30 minutes**
**Cannot be frozen**
**Serves: 4**

**Ingredients:**
**4 slices bacon**
**2 tbsp olive oil**
**400 g | 1 lb spaghetti**
**3 eggs**
**3 tbsp cream**
**100 g | 1 cup Parmesan cheese, grated**
**1 tbsp chives, chopped**
**4 cloves of garlic**

**Method:**

Cut the bacon into thin strips. Fry the bacon gently in a large skillet in two tablespoons of oil.

Cook the spaghetti in boiling, salted water for 8-9 minutes, until al dente.

Beat the eggs and cream and season with salt and pepper. Stir in ½ cup of Parmesan cheese and the chives.

Remove the crispy bacon slices from the skillet and keep warm. Peel the garlic, finely chop and gently sauté in the bacon fat.

Drain the spaghetti well, then place immediately in the skillet and toss in the bacon fat. Now take the skillet from the heat. Pour in the egg and cream mixture and stir until the spaghetti is coated with the sauce.

Mix in the bacon, season with freshly milled pepper, sprinkle the remaining Parmesan cheese over the top and serve.

# Polenta pizza with bell peppers and broccoli

**Prep and cook time: 1 hour 30 minutes**
**Can be frozen**
**Serves: 4**

**Ingredients:**
250 g | 1 ½ cups broccoli florets
3 green leek leaves
2 carrots, slices
2 tbsp sunflower oil
1 leek, thinly sliced
2 red bell peppers,
deseeded and sliced into strips
2 yellow bell peppers,
deseeded and sliced into strips
5 tbsp olive oil
3 slices crispbread, crumbled

**For the base**
250 g | 1 ¼ cups polenta

**Method:**
Bring 4½ cups water to a boil in a pan with the broccoli, leek leaves and carrots. Add the oil and a little salt and cook for 15 minutes until the vegetables are soft. Drain, retaining the cooking liquid (broth). Puree the vegetables with 1 cup of the broth.

For the topping place the leek and bell peppers in a pan with 1 cup of water and a pinch of salt. Cover, bring to a boil and cook for 7 minutes.

For the base place the vegetable broth in a pan, bring to a boil and add the polenta gradually, stirring continuously. Turn down the heat and let simmer for 25 minutes, until thickened, stirring occasionally.

Heat the oven to 220°C (200°C fan) 425°F, gas 7.

Spread the polenta over an oiled cookie sheet to a layer 1 cm / ½ in thick. Let cool.

Spread the vegetable puree over the polenta and spread the bell pepper and leek on top. Heat the olive oil and fry the crispbread crumbs until golden brown. Sprinkle over the polenta pizza.

Bake for 12-15 minutes.

# Fried halibut fillet on risotto with mushrooms and chestnuts

Prep and cook time: 1 hour 15 minutes
Cannot be frozen
Serves: 4

## Ingredients:

100 g | ¼ lb broad|fava beans
400 g | 3½ cups chestnuts, shelled
8 small halibut fillets
1 lemon, zest in strips, juice squeezed
3 tbsp light soy sauce
1 shallot, finely chopped
2 stalks celery, leaves saved
for garnishing
1 clove garlic, chopped
3 tbsp olive oil
3 tbsp butter
220 g | 1 cup risotto rice
100 ml | 7 tbsp dry white wine
500 ml | 2 cups vegetable stock
100 g | 1¼ cups mushrooms, trimmed
30 g | ⅓ cup Parmesan cheese, grated

## Method:

Heat the oven to 200°C (180°C fan) 400°F, gas 6.

Marinate the fish fillets with the lemon juice and soy sauce.

Slice half the celery very finely for the garnish. Lay the strips in ice-cold water with the lemon zest. Chop the remaining celery.

Heat 1 tbsp olive oil and 1 tbsp butter in a skillet. Fry the onion, garlic and chopped celery over a low heat for 2-3 minutes. Add the risotto rice and fry for 1-2 minutes, stirring.

Pour in the wine and half the stock and bring to a boil. Simmer the rice over a low heat for 18-20 minutes until done, but not soft. Keep adding a little stock whenever the rice has absorbed the liquid. Stir in the beans after 15 minutes.

Melt the remaining butter in a pan over a low heat. Fry the mushrooms and chestnuts gently for 3-5 minutes until golden brown. Season with salt.

Stir the Parmesan into the risotto when done and season with salt and pepper. Add the mushrooms and chestnuts. Cover and take off the heat.

Heat the remaining oil in a skillet. Lift the fish fillets out of the marinade and pat dry with kitchen paper. Fry for 5-7 minutes over a medium to high heat, turning once. Season with pepper.

Spoon the risotto onto plates and arrange the fish on top. Garnish with lemon zest, celery strips and celery leaves.

# Seafood paella

**Prep and cook time: 1 hour**
**Cannot be frozen**
**Serves: 6**

## Ingredients:

**1 onion, chopped**
**4 cloves garlic, chopped**
**400 g | 1 lb mussels, washed**
**300 g | 2 cups prawns|shrimps, peeled**
**300 g | ¾ lb calamari, ready to cook, washed, chopped**
**10 tbsp olive oil**
**4 tomatoes**
**1 handful peas, frozen**
**1 litre| 4 cups vegetable stock**
**400 g | 2 cups short grain rice**
**8 strands saffron**
**2 red bell peppers, chopped**
**2 tbsp parsley, chopped**

## Method:

Preheat oven to 200°C (180°C fan) 400°F, gas 6.

Heat 5 tbsp olive oil in a large, deep pan. Fry onion until soft. Add garlic. Pour on 2 cups of the stock and bring to a boil. Add the mussels and simmer, uncovered, for a further 10 minutes. Discard unopened mussels, remove the rest from the stock and set aside.

Heat remaining olive oil in a large paella pan and fry the rice briefly, stirring continuously. Infuse saffron in a few spoonfuls of hot stock; add to the rice with remaining stock and onion mixture. Bring to a boil and simmer for 25 minutes. Stir in bell pepper, tomatoes, peas, peeled prawns/shrimps and calamari.

Cover paella with tin foil and put it into the oven. Bake for 20 minutes. Stir in the mussels after 15 minutes, season with salt and pepper and return to oven.

Sprinkle parsley over and serve.

# Aubergine with tomato and rice stuffing

**Prep and cook time: 1 hour**
**Can be frozen**
**Serves: 4**

**Ingredients:**

**4 spring onions|scallions, cut into rings**
**200 g | ½ lb baby tomatoes**
**4 small aubergine|eggplant**
**4 tbsp olive oil**
**2 shallots, finely diced**
**2 cloves garlic, finely chopped**
**100 g | 1 cup cooked rice**
**2 tbsp tomato puree**
**1 tbsp oregano, chopped**
**80 g | ⅔ cup hard cheese, grated**

**Method:**

Heat the oven to 180°C (160°C fan) 375°F, gas 5.

Wash and slice the tomatoes. Wash and halve the aubergine/eggplants lengthwise and scrape out the flesh, keeping the skins intact. Sprinkle with plenty of salt and leave to stand for 10 minutes to draw out some of the water. Rinse and dry.

Finely chop the aubergine/eggplants flesh. Heat 2 tbsp oil and sweat the flesh with the shallot and garlic for 5 minutes, stirring. Add a little water if necessary.

Mix in the rice, spring onions/scallions, tomato puree and oregano. Season to taste with salt and pepper.

Stuff the aubergine/eggplants skins with the stuffing, sprinkle with cheese and place in a baking dish. Drizzle with a little olive oil and bake in the preheated oven for 30 minutes.

Serve with minted yoghurt and flatbread.

# Hazelnut and parsley risotto

**Prep and cook time: 40 minutes**
**Can be frozen**
**Serves: 4**

**Ingredients:**
1 tbsp butter
2 tbsp olive oil
1 onion, chopped
2 cloves garlic, chopped
300 g | 1½ cups risotto rice
1100 ml | 4½ cups vegetable stock
80 g | ¾ cup Parmesan cheese, freshly grated
4 tbsp hazelnuts (cob nuts), roughly chopped
2 tbsp parsley, chopped

**Method:**
Heat the butter and oil in a skillet and fry the onion, garlic and rice for a few minutes until transparent.

Gradually add the stock a ladle at a time, stirring constantly for 20 minutes until the rice is cooked. The risotto shouldn't be too liquid or too stodgy.

Just before serving, stir the Parmesan into the risotto and season with salt and ground pepper.

Roast the hazelnuts in a pan without fat. Serve the risotto on plates, sprinkled with cob nuts and parsley.

# Stuffed tomatoes with rice, capers and dried tomatoes

**Prep and cook time: 50 minutes**
**Cannot be frozen**
**Serves: 4**

**Ingredients:**
**8 large beef tomatoes**
**4 tbsp olive oil**
**2 onions, finely chopped**
**2 garlic cloves, finely chopped**
**40 g | 1½ cups fresh basil, half chopped**
**60 g | ¼ cup dried tomatoes, chopped**
**200 g 1 cup cooked rice**
**50 g | ½ cup black olives, pitted, finely chopped**
**2 tbsp small capers**

**Method:**

Heat the oven to 200°C (180°C fan) 400°F, gas 6.

Cut off the tomato tops to form lids. Scoop out the seeds and discard. Scoop out the flesh and chop.

Heat 1 tbsp olive oil in a pan. Stir in the onion, garlic and chopped basil and fry. Add the dried tomatoes and the tomato flesh and bring to a boil and simmer until the liquid has evaporated.

Add the rice, olives and capers. Season with salt and pepper and take off the heat.

Oil an oven-proof dish. Set the hollowed-out tomatoes in the dish. Fill the tomatoes and place the lids on.
Bake for 25 minutes.

Garnish with the remaining basil and drizzle with olive oil before serving.

# Greek mutton pilaf

**Prep and cook time: 1 hour 10 minutes**
**Can be frozen**
**Serves: 4**

**Ingredients:**
**3 tbsp sunflower oil**
**500 g | 1¼ lbs leg of mutton**
**(or lamb), chopped into cubes**
**2 onions, chopped**
**2 cloves garlic, chopped**
**600 ml | 2½ cups chicken stock**
**1 dried chilli, crushed**
**800 g | 4 cups tomatoes, chopped**
**300 g | 1½ cups short-grain rice**
**(risotto rice)**
**1 tsp dried oregano**
**fresh oregano leaves, to garnish**

**Method:**
Heat the oil in a frying pan and brown the mutton over a high heat for 4 minutes, stirring to stop the meat sticking.
Put the browned meat to one side.

Sweat the onions and garlic in the frying fat, then return the meat to the pan. Add the chicken stock and simmer gently for about 15 minutes.

Add the chilli to the pan with the tomatoes and their juice and the rice. Season with dried oregano, salt and pepper.

Cover the pilaf and cook over a low heat for 25 minutes. Stir occasionally or add a little water if the rice becomes too dry.

Serve the pilaf sprinkled with oregano.

# Pumpkin risotto with peas and pancetta

**Prep and cook time: 40 minutes**
**Cannot be frozen**
**Serves: 4**

**Ingredients:**
**12 thin slices pancetta, or streaky bacon, chopped**
**2 tbsp butter**
**1 onion, chopped**
**350 g | 2¼ cups risotto rice**
**1 small yellow pumpkin, chopped into 1 cm/½" pieces**
**100 ml | 7 tbsp white wine**
**650 ml | 2⅔ cups vegetable stock**
**150 g | 1 cup peas**
**50 g | ½ cup Parmesan cheese, finely grated**

**Method:**

Fry the pancetta in a pan over a low to medium heat for 4-6 minutes. Put aside.

Melt the butter in the bacon fat and fry the onion for 2-3 minutes until soft. Add the risotto rice and fry for 2 minutes, stirring gently. Add the pumpkin and wine.

Add the stock a ladle at a time, into the pan allowing each ladle to absorb before adding the next. This step should take 18-20 minutes until the rice is cooked but still firm. After 15 minutes, add the peas.

Just before the risotto is ready, stir in the Parmesan. Season with salt and pepper. Sprinkle the crispy pancetta on top, cover and heat through for 1-2 minutes.

# Deep-fried mozzarella risotto balls with cranberry sauce

**Prep and cook time: 1 hour**
**Cannot be frozen**
**Makes: 20 - 30**

**Ingredients:**
**500 g | 2$\frac{1}{4}$ cups risotto rice**
**500 ml | 2 cups dry white wine**
**1500 ml | 6 cups vegetable stock**
**20-30 baby mozzarella balls,**
**about 400 g (1lb)**
**400 g | 1$\frac{1}{2}$ cup cranberry sauce**
**oil for deep frying**

**Method:**
Cook the risotto rice with the wine and vegetable stock, adding the liquid a ladle at a time, until it has all been added, this step should take roughly 15-20 minutes. Then set aside and allow it to cool.

Drain the mozzarella balls on paper towels and heat the oven to 100°C (80°C fan) 200°F, gas 1.

Put a little of the cold risotto in the palm of your hand and press it flat. Put a mozzarella ball in the middle and press the risotto around it. Roll into a ball, using a little flour if it is too sticky.

Heat the oil and deep-fry the mozzarella risotto balls, a few at a time for 2-3 minutes or until golden brown. Drain on paper towels and keep warm in the oven while you fry the rest.

Serve hot with cranberry sauce.

desserts.

# Rice pudding with coconut

**Prep and cook time: 1 hour  Chilling: 2 hours**
**Cannot be frozen**
**Serves: 4**

**Ingredients:**
**300 ml | 1¹/₃ cups milk**
**200 ml | ⁷/₈ cup coconut milk**
**2 tbsp shredded coconut**
**100 g | ¹/₂ cup short-grain rice**
**70 g | ³/₈ cup sugar**
**2 eggs, separated**

**To garnish:**
**80 g | ³/₄ cup shredded coconut**
**physalis**

**Method:**

Reserve 4 tbsp of the milk. Bring the remaining milk to a boil with the coconut milk and shredded coconut. Add the rice and sugar. Cover and simmer gently for 40 minutes on a low heat until the rice is soft. Take off the heat.

Beat the egg yolks with the reserved milk and stir into the rice while still hot. Allow it to cool, stirring occasionally.

Beat the egg whites until stiff and fold into the cool rice. Spoon into 4 bowls and chill in the fridge for 1 hour.

To garnish, roast the shredded coconut without fat, stirring continually. Allow to cool and sprinkle over the puddings. Garnish with physalis and serve.

# Plum pie with crème anglaise

**Prep and cook time: 1 hour 10 minutes  Chilling time: 1 hour**
**Cannot be frozen**
**Serves: 8 - 10**

**Ingredients:**
**For the pie:**
300 g | 1¼ cups plain|all purpose flour
200 g | 1 cup butter
1 egg
100 g | 1⅛ cups sugar
a pinch of salt
500 g | 1¼ lbs plums
cinnamon
sugar

**For the crème anglaise:**
250 ml | 1 cup milk
250 ml | 1 cup cream
1 vanilla pod
5 egg yolks
60 g | ½ cup sugar

**Method:**

Cut the butter into the flour, salt and sugar. Add the egg and knead to a dough, adding a little water if the mix is too dry. Wrap in cling film and chill for 1 hour.

Heat the oven to 200°C (180°C fan) 400°F, gas 6.

Wash and dry the plums, then halve, stone and cut into wedges.

Halve the dough and roll out into 2 circles on a floured work surface. Butter the pie dish and line with one of the pastry circles. Prick with a fork.

Arrange the plums on the pastry and sprinkle with sugar and 2 tsp cinnamon. Lay the second pastry circle on top and pinch the edges together. Cut off any excess pastry. Sprinkle with sugar and bake in the hot oven for 30 minutes, until golden brown.

For the crème anglaise, scrape the seeds from the vanilla bean and add to the milk and cream. Bring to the boil, then remove from the heat.

Beat the egg yolks and sugar together in a bowl. Slowly stir the warm milk into the egg yolk mixture in a thin stream, then return to the pan and beat over a very low heat until it thickens. Do not let it boil.

Pour the custard into a jug or sauce-boat, sprinkle the surface lightly with sugar to prevent a skin from forming and let cool. Serve with the warm pie.

# Tiramisù

**Prep and cook time: 30 minutes**
**Cannot be frozen**
**Serves: 4**

**Ingredients:**
**5 egg yolks**
**50 g | ½ cup icing|confectioners' sugar**
**500 g | 2 cups mascarpone**
**40 ml | 4 tbsp almond liqueur**
**16 lady fingers (sponge fingers)**
**500 ml | 2 cups strong espresso**
**cocoa powder, for dusting**
**icing|confectioners' sugar, for dusting**

**Method:**

Beat the egg yolks and icing/confectioners' sugar until foam then stir in the mascarpone and the liqueur.

Put the espresso in a flat dish, dip half of the sponge fingers in the espresso and lay on the base of a rectangular serving dish.

Spread with half of the egg/cream mixture and dust with cocoa. Repeat the process with the remaining sponge fingers and mascarpone cream. Dust with cocoa and icing/confectioners' sugar before serving.

# Eton mess

**Prep and cook time: 25 minutes**
**Cannot be frozen**
**Serves: 4**

**Ingredients:**
**20 ml | 4 tsp kirsch**
**400 g | 3 cups strawberries,**
**hulled and quartered**
**4 tbsp sugar**
**200 ml | ⁷⁄₈ cup whipping cream**
**40 g | 4 cups meringue, crumbled**
**4 scoops vanilla ice-cream**

**To garnish:**
**mint sprigs**

**Method:**

Drizzle the kirsch over the strawberries. Sprinkle 2 tbsp sugar over and let them marinate for 30 minutes.

Lightly whip the cream and stir in the remaining sugar. Puree the strawberries in the blender. Mix the crushed meringues with the cream and sugar.

To serve, place a scoop of vanilla ice-cream in 4 tall dessert or wine glasses. Add a small spoon of cream/meringue mix to each, then half of the strawberries. Add the remaining meringue crumbs and strawberry puree. Top with the remaining cream and garnish each glass with a mint sprig.

# California cheesecake with crème fraiche topping

**Prep and cook time: 2 hours**
**Cannot be frozen**
**Serves: 8 - 10**

**Ingredients:**
**For the base:**
**100 g | ½ cup butter**
**200 g | 2 cups digestive biscuits, crushed**
**1 pinch cinnamon**
**1 tbsp sugar**

**For the cream cheese filling:**
**4 eggs**
**200 g | 1 cup sugar**
**800 g | 3½ cups cream cheese**
**2 tbsp lemon juice**

**For the topping:**
**150 g | 1½ cups crème fraiche**
**1 tbsp icing|confectioners' sugar**
**½ vanilla pod**

**Method:**
Heat the oven to 160°C (140°C fan) 325°F, gas 3.

For the base, melt the butter and set aside. Mix the crumbs with the cinnamon and sugar, add to the butter and mix well.

Line the pan with baking parchment. Spoon in the crumbed mixture and press flat.

For the filling beat the eggs with the sugar until creamy. Beat in the cream cheese and the lemon juice. Spread the mixture over the base and bake for 1 hour.

For the topping, scrape out the seeds from the vanilla pod and mix with the crème fraiche and icing/confectioners' sugar. Spread over the top of the cake and return to the oven for a further 10 minutes.

Let cool slightly in the pan. Take out of the pan, cut into slices and serve.

# Mousse au chocolat

**Prep and cook time: 30 minutes  Chilling time: 3 hours**
**Can be frozen**
**Serves: 4**

**Ingredients:**
150 g | 1 cup milk chocolate, chopped
100 g | ⅔ cup dark chocolate
70% cocoa, chopped
1 egg
1 egg yolk
2 tbsp icing|confectioners' sugar
40 ml | 8 tsp whiskey
400 ml | 1 ⅔ cups cream

**To garnish:**
2 tbsp dark chocolate,
70% cocoa, grated

**Method:**
Put the milk and dark chocolate into a bowl and place over a pan of simmering water, stirring occasionally.

Put the egg, egg yolk and sugar into a bowl over a pan of simmering water and beat until thick and creamy. Stir in the chocolate and the whiskey and leave to cool down slightly.

Whip the cream until stiff and carefully fold into the cooled chocolate cream.

Spoon the mixture into glasses and chill for 3 hours.
Serve sprinkled with grated chocolate.

# Apple pie

**Prep and cook time: 60 minutes**
**Cannot be frozen**
**Serves: 8 - 10**

**Ingredients:**
**For the pastry:**
**250 g | 2 cups plain|all purpose flour**
**½ tsp salt**
**100 g | ½ cup sugar**
**100 g | ½ cup butter, chopped**
**125 ml | ½ cup milk**

**For the filling:**
**2 tbsp fine dried breadcrumbs**
**1 kg | 2 pounds sour apples, peeled,**
**cored and chopped into eighths**
**2 tbsp lemon juice**
**50 g | ¼ cup sugar**
**½ tsp cinnamon**

**To garnish:**
**sugar**

**Method:**
Heat the oven to 180°C (160°C fan) 375°F, gas 5.

For the pastry, mix the flour with the salt and sugar. Cut in the butter and gently knead to form a dough, adding enough milk so the pastry is smooth but not sticky.

Divide the pastry into 2 and roll out both pieces. Butter the pan and line it with half of the pastry. Sprinkle with breadcrumbs.

For the filling, mix the apple pieces with the lemon juice, sugar and cinnamon and place them on the pastry base.
Lay the second pastry piece over the apple. Press the edges together well.

Bake the pie for 40 minutes until golden brown. Sprinkle with a little sugar and serve lukewarm.

**181**

# Crème caramel

**Prep and cook time: 45 minutes**
**Cannot be frozen**
**Serves: 4**

**Ingredients:**
50 g | ¼ cup sugar
2 egg yolks
1 egg
200 ml | ⅞ cup milk
150 ml | ⅔ cup cream
1/2 tsp vanilla extract

**For the caramel:**
80 g | ⅓ cup sugar

**Also needed:**
4 small pans, 150 ml / ⅔ cup capacity

**Method:**

Heat the oven to 180°C (160°C fan) 375°F, gas 5.

Beat the sugar with the egg and egg yolks. Bring the milk and cream with the vanilla extract to a boil, then pour into the egg mixture, stirring all the time.

For the caramel, simmer the sugar with 2 tbsp water in a small saucepan until the sugar is golden brown. Oil the pans slightly and pour in the caramel, tipping the bowls until the caramel is evenly spread.

Sieve the egg mixture and pour it into the bowls. Place the bowls into a large ovenproof dish or pan and fill it with water to halfway up the sides of the pan. Bake for 30 minutes until set.

Let the cream cool, keep them in the refrigerator until ready to serve.

# Lemon meringue pie

**Prep and cook time: 2 hours  Resting: 1 hour**
**Cannot be frozen**
**Serves: 8 - 10**

**Ingredients:**
**For the pastry:**
**250 g | 2 cups plain|all purpose flour**
**75 g | 3/8 cup sugar**
**1 egg yolk**
**1 pinch salt**
**125 g | 1/2 cup cold butter**
**beans, for baking blind**

**For the filling:**
**5 eggs, separated**
**100 g | 1/2 cup sugar**
**400 ml | 1 2/3 cups condensed milk, sweetened**
**125 ml | 1/2 cup lemon juice, freshly pressed**
**1 tsp lemon zest, grated**
**1 pinch salt**
**1 tsp baking powder**

**Method:**
Cut the butter into the pastry ingredients and knead lightly to form a dough, add a little cold water if the mixture is too dry. Shape to a ball, wrap in cling film and chill in the fridge for 1 hour.

Heat the oven to 180°C (160°C fan) 375°F, gas 5.

Roll out the pastry onto a floured board. Butter the pie pan and line it with the pastry, making a rim. Line the pastry with baking parchment and scatter beans on it.

Bake the pastry case blind for 15-20 minutes. Take off the beans and parchment and let cool completely.

For the filling, beat the egg yolks with 2 tbsp of the sugar until thick and creamy, adding the condensed milk. Add the lemon juice and zest, mix well and spread evenly over the pastry case.

Turn the oven down to 160°C and bake the lemon pie for 30 minutes. Meanwhile beat the egg whites with the salt and baking powder until stiff. Gradually add the rest of the sugar and beat until stiff once more.

Take the pie out of the oven and spread the egg white lightly on top of the lemon filling. Bake the pie for a further 10 minutes until golden brown.

# Vanilla blancmange with berry sauce

**Prep and cook time: 25 minutes  Chilling: 4 hours**
**Cannot be frozen**
**Serves: 4**

**Ingredients:**
**For the blancmange:**
**6 sheets white gelatine**
**500 ml | 2 cups cream**
**grated zest of 1 lemon**
**1/2 tsp vanilla extract**
**75 g | 3/8 cup sugar**

**For the sauce:**
**400 g | 3-4 cups fresh berries**
**25 g | 1/8 cup sugar**

**Method:**

For the blancmange, soften the gelatine in cold water. Bring the cream to a boil with the lemon zest, the vanilla extract and sugar and then remove from the heat.

Squeeze out the gelatine and dissolve it in the hot cream, stirring.

Spoon the mixture into the moulds and let cool. Then chill in the refrigerator for at least 3 hours until set.

For the sauce, bring half of the berries to a boil in a pan with the sugar. Set the berries aside to cool them slightly, then puree and press through a sieve. Add the remaining berries and let cool.

To serve, turn the puddings onto dessert plates and drizzle over the cold berry sauce.

# Bread and butter pudding

**Prep and cook time: 1 hour**
**Can be frozen**
**Serves: 4**

**Ingredients:**
50 g | 1/3 cup raisins
40 ml | 8 tsp brandy
40 g | 1/4 cup butter
400 g | 1 lb day-old white bread,
in thick slices
200 ml | 7/8 cup cream
200 ml | 7/8 cup milk
3 eggs
2 tbsp icing|confectioners' sugar
1 tsp vanilla extract
2 1/2 cm cinnamon
2 tbsp demerara sugar
2 tbsp ground hazelnuts (cob nuts)

**Method:**

Heat the oven to 200°C (180°C fan) 400°F, gas 6.

Soak the raisins in the brandy.

Spread butter thickly on the slices of bread and lay in overlapping rows in an ovenproof dish. Sprinkle the raisins over the bread.

Beat the cream with the milk, eggs, icing/confectioners' sugar, vanilla extract and cinnamon. Pour over the bread slices. Let it stand for 10 minutes.

Mix the demerara sugar with the hazelnuts and sprinkle over the softened bread. Cover with tin foil and bake for 20 minutes.

Take off the foil and bake for a further 20 minutes until golden brown.

Spoon onto plates and serve with custard or cream

# Banoffee pie

**Prep and cook time: 50 minutes**
**Cannot be frozen**
**Serves: 8 - 10**

**Ingredients:**
**For the base:**
250 g | 2 cups plain|all purpose flour
50 g | ¼ cup sugar
125 g | 1 cup butter

**For the filling:**
125 g | 1 cup sugar
250 ml | 1 cup cream
3-4 bananas (depending on size), peeled and sliced lengthways
lemon juice, to brush on
300 ml | 1⅓ cups cream, whipped

**To garnish:**
pecan nuts
white chocolate, shavings

**Method:**

For the pastry, mix the flour with the sugar, add the butter in pieces and knead quickly to form a dough. Roll it out to a 5mm thickness and line the pan with the pastry, making a 2-3 cm / 1" high rim. Chill in the pan for 30 minutes.

Heat the oven to 180°C (160°C fan) 375°F, gas 5.

Bake the pie case for 20-30 minutes. Take out and allow it to cool.

For the filling, melt the sugar and let it caramelize slightly. Pour on the cream, bring to a boil and let boil until the mixture is reduced to a thick consistency. Allow it to cool slightly.

Brush the sliced bananas with lemon juice and lay in the pastry case. Pour the caramel cream over the bananas and allow it to cool completely in the fridge.

To serve, spread the whipped cream over the pie and garnish with pecan nuts and chocolate shavings.

# Pears in a pastry case

**Prep and cook time: 45 minutes**
**Cannot be frozen**
**Serves: 4**

**Ingredients:**
**400 g | 1 lb puff pastry**
**4 pears, peeled, cored (but leave whole with the stems on)**
**2 tbsp lemon juice**
**2 egg yolks, beaten**
**40 g | ½ cup cream**
**3-4 tbsp raspberry jam (jelly)**

**To serve:**
**vanilla ice-cream**

**Method:**
Heat the oven to 180°C (160°C fan) 375°F, gas 5.

Drizzle the pears with the lemon juice and pour the cream over them.

Roll out the pastry and cut out four squares 15 cm x 15 cm / 6 x 6" each. Cut a thin strip off each square to decorate.

Place each pear in the middle of a pastry square.
Pull up the sides and press together firmly (leaving the stalk sticking out). Brush with beaten egg yolk and decorate with the remaining pastry.

Line a cookie sheet with baking parchment. Place the pears on the cookie sheet and bake for 15-20 minutes until golden brown. Meanwhile heat the raspberry jam and press through a sieve.

Take the pears out and allow to cool for a few minutes, before serving with the raspberry sauce and vanilla ice-cream.

# Strawberry shortcake

**Prep and cook time: 1 hour**
**Cannot be frozen**
**Serves: 6**

**Ingredients:**
**For the filling:**
**800 g | 6 cups fresh strawberries, hulled**
**6 tbsp granulated sugar**

**For the shortcakes:**
**200 g | 2 cups plain|all purpose flour**
**½ tbsp table salt**
**1 tbsp baking powder**
**3 tbsp sugar**
**100 g | ½ cup butter, frozen**
**1 egg, beaten**
**125 ml | ½ cup cream**
**1 egg white, lightly beaten**
**1 tbsp sugar for sprinkling**
**icing|confectioners' sugar, for dusting**

**For the topping:**
**250 ml | 1 cup cream**
**1 tbsp sugar**
**1 tbsp vanilla extract**

**Method:**

Crush half the strawberries with a potato masher or fork and quarter the remaining. Sprinkle with the sugar and set aside while preparing the shortcakes.

Heat oven to 220°C (200°C fan) 425°F, gas 7.

Mix flour, salt, baking powder and sugar in medium bowl. Grate the butter into dry ingredients and cut in with a knife until the mixture resembles breadcrumbs.

Mix the beaten egg with half-and-half, pour into the flour mixture and toss with a fork until large clumps form.
Turn the mixture onto a floured work surface and lightly knead until it comes together.

Roll the dough to a thickness of about 2½ cm / 1". Using a 7 cm / 2 ¾" cookie cutter, cut 6 dough rounds and place on a cookie sheet lined with baking parchment. Brush the dough tops with egg white and sprinkle with remaining sugar.

Bake until golden brown for 12 to 14 minutes. Place the cookie on a wire rack and allow to cool for 10 minutes.

Whip the cream with the sugar and vanilla extract until nearly doubled in volume and forming soft peaks.

Split each shortcake crosswise by hand, spoon a portion of berries and then a dollop of whipped cream over each cake bottom. Cap with a cake top, dust with icing/confectioners' sugar, if desired. Serve immediately.

# Steamed date pudding with chocolate sauce

**Prep and cook time: 2 hour 40 minutes**
**Cannot be frozen**
**Serves: 4**

**Ingredients:**
50 g | ¼ cup dried dates, finely chopped
1 tsp baking powder
40 g | ⅛ cup soft butter
50 g | ¼ cup sugar
1 egg
1 tbsp lemon juice
2 tbsp rum
60 g | ½ cup plain|all purpose flour
1 tsp ground cinnamon
½ tsp salt
50 g | ⅓ cup walnuts, chopped
50 g | ⅓ cup raisins

**For the sauce:**
100 g | ¼ lb dark chocolate, 70% cocoa
2 tbsp cream
2 tbsp espresso

**Method:**

Butter the bowls well. Take a saucepan large enough to set all the bowls on the base. Line the base with a folded tea towel, fill with water to about half the height of the bowls and slowly bring to a boil.

Mix the dates with the baking powder. Beat the butter with the sugar until creamy. Beat in the egg, lemon juice and rum very thoroughly. Add the flour, cinnamon and salt and mix well. Finally mix in the dates, nuts and raisins.

Spoon the dough into the bowls, cover with lids or aluminium foil and place onto the cloth in the pan. Cover the saucepan and steam over a low heat for 2 hours. You may need to add more water to the pan to prevent it boiling dry.

For the sauce, melt the chocolate slowly in a bowl over a pan of simmering water. Stir in the cream and espresso. Allow it to cool slightly.

Take the puddings off the heat and let them stand for 5 minutes. Loosen the puddings in the bowls by running a sharp knife around the rim. Turn out them and serve warm or at room temperature, pouring over the warm sauce.

# Rhubarb crumble with crème anglaise

**Prep and cook time: 1 hour  Chilling time: 1 hour**
**Cannot be frozen**
**Serves: 4**

**Ingredients:**
**200 g | 1²/₃ cups plain|all purpose flour**
**100 g | ²/₃ cup chopped hazelnuts**
**(cob nuts)**
**150 g | ³/₄ cup sugar**
**1 egg yolk**
**150 g | ²/₃ cup soft butter**
**500 g | 5 cups rhubarb, peeled**
**and chopped into chunks**

**For the crème anglaise:**
**200 ml | ⁷/₈ cup milk**
**200 ml | ⁷/₈ cup cream**
**1 vanilla pod, split open,**
**seeds scraped out**
**5 egg yolks**
**75 g | ³/₈ cup sugar**

**Method:**

Heat the oven to 220°C (200°C fan) 425°F, gas 7.

Mix the flour, hazelnuts and 100g / ½ cup sugar. Rub in the egg yolk and butter by hand to make the crumble.

Place ²/₃ of the crumble in a greased dish and press down firmly to form the base. Chill for 1 hour.

Place the rhubarb on the base and sprinkle the remaining sugar over. Top with the remaining crumble.
Bake for 30 minutes until golden brown.

For the crème anglaise, scrape out the seeds from the vanilla bean, add them to the milk and cream in a small pan and gently bring to a boil. Beat the egg yolks with the sugar in a bowl until thick and creamy.

Stir the hot cream and milk into the egg yolks, return to the pan and stir continuously over a very low heat; do not boil.

Sieve the crème anglaise, stirring occasionally.
Serve with the crumble.

# Pecan pie with pumpkin

**Prep and cook time: 1 hour 40 minutes**
**Can be frozen**
**Serves: 8 - 10**

**Ingredients:**
**For the dough:**
200 g | 1²/₃ cups plain|all purpose flour
1 pinch salt
100 g | ½ cup cold butter
1 egg
flour, for working
dried beans, for baking blind

**For the filling:**
400 g | 2¼ cups pumpkin or squash,
peeled and chopped
2 eggs, lightly beaten
180 g | ¾ cup cane sugar
2-3 tbsp plain|all purpose flour
1 tsp ground cinnamon
½ tsp ground ginger
1 pinch nutmeg
½ tsp salt
120 ml | ½ cup cream

**For the nut mixture:**
1 tbsp butter
60 g | ¼ cup cane sugar
½ tbsp orange zest, grated
100 g | ½ cup pecan nuts,
chopped roughly

**To decorate:**
pecan nuts
icing|confectioners' sugar

**Method:**
For the dough, heap the flour on the work surface. Mix with the salt and make a well in the middle. Place the cold butter in small pieces around the well and break the egg into the middle. Add 4 tsp lukewarm water and chop the ingredients with a knife to form crumbs. Knead quickly by hand to a dough and shape into a ball. Wrap in cling film and chill for 30 minutes.

Cook the pumpkin in boiling water for 15 minutes. Drain, allow it to cool and puree.

Heat the oven to 200°C (180°C fan) 400°F, gas 6.

Grease the pie dish. Roll out the pastry on a floured surface and line the dish with it. Place baking parchment on the pastry, weight with beans and bake blind for 15 minutes. Take out of the oven, remove the parchment and beans and let cool.

For the filling, beat the eggs with the sugar, flour, cinnamon, ginger, nutmeg and salt. Gradually stir in the squash puree and the cream. Spread the filling in the pastry case and bake for 30 minutes.

For the nut mixture, melt the butter. Mix with the sugar, orange zest and chopped nuts. Spread on top of the pie and bake for 10 more minutes. Allow the pie to cool

Decorate with the pecan nuts and dust with icing/confectioners' sugar to serve.

# Raspberry trifle with vanilla sauce

**Prep and cook time: 30 minutes  Chilling at least: 4 hours**
**Cannot be frozen**
**Serves: 4**

**Ingredients:**
**For the vanilla sauce:**
**20 g | 1 tbsp cornflour|cornstarch**
**2 egg yolks**
**40 g $^1/_4$ cup sugar**
**250 ml | 1 cup milk**
**$^1/_2$ tsp vanilla extract**
**200 ml | $^7/_8$ cup cream**

**For the trifle:**
**200 g | $^1/_2$ lb lady fingers**
**or boudoir biscuits**
**2 tbsp raspberry jelly**
**2 tbsp grenadine syrup**
**40 ml | 8 tsp dry sherry**
**2 ml orange liqueur**
**100 g | $^7/_8$ cup fresh raspberries,**
**stalks removed**
**100 g | $^1/_2$ cup fresh strawberries,**
**hulled and quartered**

**To garnish:**
**chocolate almonds, roughly chopped**

**Method:**

For the sauce, beat the cornflour/cornstarch, egg yolks and half the sugar with $^1/_2$ cup cold milk. Bring the remaining milk to a boil with the vanilla extract and the remaining sugar.

Take the milk off the heat and stir the egg yolk mixture into the hot milk. Return to the heat and continue to stir the sauce vigorously until it thickens, do not let it boil. Remove from the heat and allow it to cool, stirring occasionally.

Whip the cream until stiff. Stir half of it into the sauce, when cool.

Crumble the lady fingers coarsely and place them in 4 large glasses. Mix the jelly with the grenadine syrup and sherry. Drizzle the orange liqueur over the berries.

Spoon the jelly onto the biscuits. Fill the glasses with the berries and cover with the sauce. Top with the remaining cream and place in the fridge for at least 4 hours for the flavours to mingle.

Garnish with the chocolate almonds and serve.

# Ice-cream gateau with lime mousse and cream

**Prep and cook time: 50 minutes  Chilling and freezing time: 12 hours**
**Can be frozen**
**Serves: 8 - 10**

**Ingredients:**
**For the base:**
140 g | ¾ cup butter
250 g | 2½ cups digestive
biscuits, crushed
2 tbsp icing|confectioners' sugar

**For the filling:**
8 limes
600 ml | 2½ cups condensed milk
10 sheets white gelatine
6 egg yolks
150 g | ¾ cup sugar
200 ml | ⅞ cup cream

**For the topping:**
100 g | ½ cup sugar
600 ml | 2½ cups cream

**Method:**
Melt the butter in a small pan. Put the biscuit crumbs into a bowl and mix with the butter and icing/confectioners' sugar.

Line the base of a spring-form pan with baking parchment. Press the crumb mixture firmly onto the base and sides of the pan using the back of a tablespoon, making the sides 4 cm / 1½" high. Put into the fridge for 3 hours until firm.

Wash the limes in hot water and dry. Finely grate the rind. Squeeze all the limes and measure 250 ml / 1 cup juice. Soak the gelatine in plenty of cold water.

Put the lime juice, grated rind and condensed milk into a medium size pan and heat gently. Whisk the egg yolks and sugar in a large bowl until pale and fluffy, using the whisk of an electric mixer. Add the lime and condensed mixture, return to the pan and gently bring to a boil, stirring.

Pour the mixture into a clean bowl and stir in the squeezed-out gelatine. Chill the mixture for 2-3 hours, stirring occasionally. As soon as the mixture begins set stir in the whipped cream. Spread the lime mousse on the crumb base and smooth the top, then put the cake into the fridge for a further 3 hours.

For the topping, whip the cream stiffly with the sugar and pile on top of the lime mousse to form a dome. Fluff up the surface with a spoon if you wish. Place the gateau into the freezer for 3-4 hours until the cream is slightly frozen.

Transfer the gateau from the freezer to the fridge 30 minutes before cutting. Then carefully loosen from the sides of the spring-form pan with a sharp knife and lift the cake onto a large serving plate.

# Lemon posset

**Prep and cook time: 10 minutes  Chilling at least: 3 hours**
**Cannot be frozen**
**Serves: 4**

**Ingredients:**
**400 ml | 1²/₃ cups heavy cream**
**120 g | ⁵/₈ cup sugar**
**2 lemons, juice and zest**

**Method:**

Bring the double cream to a boil, stirring all the time. Let it simmer gently for 3 minutes.

Take off the heat and stir in the sugar, lemon juice and zest, retaining a little zest to garnish.

Spoon into 4 small bowls and sprinkle the remaining zest over.

Chill for at least 3 hours before serving.

# Cherry clafoutis

**Prep and cook time: 1 hour  Chilling: 30 minutes**
**Can be frozen**
**Serves: 8 - 10**

**Ingredients:**
**4 eggs**
**75 g | ³/₈ cup sugar**
**80 g | ²/₃ cup plain|all purpose flour**
**1 pinch salt**
**1 pinch baking powder**
**100 g | ²/₃ cup quark (low-fat soft cheese)**
**75 ml | ¹/₃ cup milk**
**750 g | 4¹/₂ cups cherries, pitted**

**To decorate:**
**icing|confectioners' sugar**

**Method:**

Beat the eggs with the sugar until thick and creamy. Beat in the flour, salt, baking powder, quark and milk. Chill in the fridge for 30 minutes.

Heat the oven to 200°C (180°C fan) 400°F, gas 6.

Butter the pan. Spoon in ¹/₃ of the dough and arrange half of the cherries on it. Spoon on the remaining dough, smooth and sprinkle the remaining cherries on top.

Bake for 30-40 minutes. Sprinkle with icing/confectioners' sugar and serve.

# Nut brownies with fudge frosting

**Prep and cook time: 1 hour**
**Cannot be frozen**
**Makes: 12**

**Ingredients:**
**For the brownies:**
150 g | 1 cup cups dark chocolate, 70% cocoa
125 g | ½ cup soft butter
150 g | 1½ cups cane sugar
2 eggs
100 g | ¾ cup plain|all purpose flour
½ tsp baking powder
150 g | ⅞ cup chopped walnuts

**For the frosting:**
100 ml | 7 tbsp cream
250 g | 2 cups milk chocolate

**Method:**
Heat the oven to 200°C (180°C fan) 400°F, gas 6.

Melt the dark chocolate in a bowl over a pan of simmering water, stirring continually. Let cool slightly.

Beat the butter and sugar in a bowl until creamy. Beat in the eggs gradually, then add the chocolate. Mix the flour, baking powder and walnuts; stir them into the chocolate mixture.

Butter a brownie tin and sprinkle it with flour. Pour the mixture into the brownie tin, smooth it and bake for 30 minutes. Turn out onto a wire rack to cool.

For the frosting, pour the cream into a bowl. Add the chocolate and melt in a bowl over a pan of simmering water, stirring. Allow it to cool, stirring occasionally. Spread over the brownies and place in the refrigerator to set.

# ice-cream filled apple pie with crème anglaise

**Prep and cook time: 2 hours 20 minutes**
**Cannot be frozen**
**Serves: 4**

**Ingredients:**
**For the pastry:**
200 g | 2 cups plain|all purpose flour
1 pinch salt
2 tbsp sugar
125 g | ⅝ cup cold butter
1 egg

**For the apple puree:**
1 kg | 2 lbs 4 large cooking apples
150 g | ¾ cup sugar
1 lemon, juiced
1 tbsp butter

**For the ice-cream filling:**
40 ml | 8 tsp Calvados
4 tbsp crème fraiche
2 tbsp yoghurt

**To garnish:**
1 large apple
1 egg white
2½ tbsp sugar

**For the crème anglaise:**
1 vanilla pod, sliced open
250 ml | 1 cup milk
125 ml | ½ cup cream
3 egg yolks
100 g | ½ cup sugar

**Method:**

For the pastry, chop all the ingredients with a knife and then quickly knead to form a dough with your hands, form into a ball, and chill for 30 minutes. Roll the pastry out to a thickness of about 2-3 mm on a floured work surface. Cut out 4 circles for the lids, then grease the rings.

Line the bottom and sides of greased rings with the remaining pastry. Fill each ring with pulses. Put small heaps of pulses on lined cookie sheet and lay the pastry circle lids over them. The pastry will mould to the shape of the pulses during baking.

For the apple puree, heat the butter in a frying pan, add the apples, lemon juice and sugar and cook over a medium heat until the apples soften. Take out about half the cooked apples and puree.

For the ice-cream filling, mix the apple puree with the Calvados, crème fraiche and yoghurt. Fill 4 metal rings 7 cm / 2¾" diameter x 4 cm / 1½" deep with the ice-cream and freeze until firm.

Bake the pastry for 20 minutes (200°C (180°C fan) 400°F, gas 6), until golden brown. Remove the pulses from the rings but leave the pastry cases to cool slightly. Leave the lids on top of the pulses to cool.

For the garnish wash, quarter and core the apple and cut into wedges. Sauté in butter for 2-3 minutes, until golden brown, then sprinkle with sugar and caramelise. If the caramel

For the crème anglaise, see page 214.

Heat the reserved apple puree and spread a little on the base of each pastry case, put the ice-cream on top and cover with more apple puree. Put on the lids and serve with caramelised apples and crème anglaise.

# Raspberry jelly with crème anglaise and fresh raspberries

**Prep and cook time: 20 minutes  Marinating time: 1 hours  Chilling time: 4 hours**
**Cannot be frozen**
**Serves: 4**

**Ingredients:**
**500 g | 4 cups raspberries**
**80 g | ⅓ cup sugar**
**3 tbsp lemon juice**
**5 sheets white gelatine**
**2 sheets red gelatine**
**500 ml | 2 cups raspberry juice,**
**apple juice may be used instead**

**For the crème anglaise:**
**1 vanilla pod, sliced open**
**250 ml | 1 cup milk**
**125 ml | ½ cup cream**
**3 egg yolks**
**100 g | ½ cup sugar**

**Method:**

Marinate 400g / 3½ cups raspberries with the sugar and lemon juice for 1 hour, reserving 100 g / ½ cup for the jelly and for decoration.

Soften the gelatine in cold water. Puree half the marinated raspberries, pass through a sieve and mix with the raspberry juice.

Squeeze the gelatine and dissolve with a little of the raspberry liquid in a bowl set it over a pan of simmering water. Add the remaining raspberry liquid and stir until cool.

Pour the jelly into 4 moistened jelly moulds and place in the refrigerator for 4 hours. Check frequently after about half an hour and when the mixture starts to gel press in half the reserved raspberries.

For the crème anglaise, gently heat the split vanilla pod with the milk and cream. After 5 minutes, remove the vanilla pod. In a separate bowl, beat the egg yolks and sugar until white and fluffy. Gradually pour the hot milk in a thin stream into the egg mixture and beat in a bowl over a pan of simmering water until thick and creamy.

Dip the jelly moulds quickly into hot water. Turn out and drizzle over the crème anglaise. Garnish with raspberries and serve.

# Sticky toffee pudding

**Prep and cook time: 1 hour 20 minutes**
**Can be frozen**
**Serves: 4**

**Ingredients:**
75 g | ½ cup prunes
50 g | ⅓ cup pitted dates
50 g | ⅓ cup raisins
½ tsp baking soda
60 g | ¼ cup soft butter
175 g | ⅞ cup brown sugar
1 egg
225 g | 2 cups plain|all purpose flour
2½ cm cinnamon
½ tsp cocoa powder
2½ cm vanilla seeds
1 tsp baking powder

**For the sauce:**
150 ml | ⅔ cup cream
50 g | ½ cup dark chocolate,
70% cocoa
80g sugar
20 ml | 4 tsp whiskey

**Method:**

Pour 250 ml / 1 cup boiling water over the prunes, dates and raisins. Allow them to soak for 1 hour. Drain, reserving the liquid.

Heat the oven to 180°C (160°C fan) 375°F, gas 5.

Chop the fruit roughly and set aside 2 tbsp for the sauce. Dissolve the baking soda in the soaking liquid.

Beat the butter with the sugar until white and creamy. Beat in the egg. Mix the flour, cinnamon, cocoa, vanilla seeds, baking soda liquid and baking powder; beat this mixture into the butter.

Stir in the drained fruit and spoon the dough into the buttered ovenproof bowl. Cover tightly and stand in a deep roasting pan, add water to half the height of the bowl and steam in oven for 35-40 minutes.

For the sauce heat the sugar, cream until boiling, remove from the heat and melt the chocolate in the cream, stirring continuously. Mix in the whiskey and the reserved fruit and let the sauce cool.

To serve, turn the warm pudding out of the bowl, slice and serve with the sauce and either ice-cream or custard.

# Mini-cheesecakes with cherry sauce

**Prep and cook time: 1 hour  Chilling time: 12 hours**
**Cannot be frozen**
**Serves: 4**

**Ingredients:**
**For the sponge base:**
50 g | ¼ cup soft butter, or margarine
50 g | ¼ cup sugar
50 g | ½ cup self-raising flour
¼ tsp baking powder
1 egg

**For the topping:**
300 g | 1¼ cup full-fat cream cheese
50 g | ¼ cup sugar
1 lemon, grated rind and juice of half
2 eggs, beaten
120 ml | ½ cup whipping cream

**In addition:**
350 g | 1¾ cups red cherries,
halved and pips removed
3 tbsp sugar

**Method:**
Preheat the oven to 180°C (160°C fan) 375°F, gas 5.

Place all the sponge ingredients into a bowl or food processor and beat until smooth.

Divide between individually lined cans and smooth flat. Bake for 8-10 minutes until well risen and the tops spring back when lightly pressed with a fingertip.

Beat the cream cheese, sugar and lemon rind together. Gradually mix in the juice of half the lemon, the beaten eggs and cream, until smooth. Pour the cream cheese mixture into the tins. Reduce the oven temperature to 160°C and cook for 25 minutes or until just set. Turn off the oven and let cool with the door slightly ajar for 30 minutes.

When cool, transfer the cans to the fridge and leave overnight, or for at least 3 hours before serving. Remove the tins and paper from the cheesecakes.

Gently heat the cherries in a pan with the sugar for five minutes, until the sauce thickens and the cherries begin to soften. Remove and allow the mixture to cool. Pour over the cheesecakes when serving.

# index

# index.

# index.